# STAR DELIVERANCE

*A Divine Manual for Protecting Your Prophetic Rank and Reclaiming Your Destiny from Spiritual Thieves*

Dr. Philomena Gerald

# PREFACE

The world is currently navigating a "cultural fog" so dense that many have lost sight of the true north. In our modern marketplace, leadership is often reduced to a set of soft skills, and parenting is frequently seen as a series of survival tactics. But for those called to govern, there is a higher requirement.

This book was born out of a realization that true influence is not something you "do"; it is something you **occupy**. It is a recognition that every individual is designed to function as a **Fixed Star** in the firmament of their industry, their community, and their home. A star does not argue with the night; it simply shines, and in doing so, it provides the navigation necessary for everyone within its reach to find their way home.

As a writer, my goal was to provide a manual, a **Standard of Holiness**, that bridges the gap between spiritual authority and practical execution. Whether you are leading a boardroom, a classroom, or a household, the principles of **Navigational Governance** remain the same: your stability is the safety of those who follow you.

In these chapters, we move from the constitutional framework of your purpose to the fierce, protective mandate of the **Mother of Lions**. We explore the "Judicial Preservation" of your reputation and the mechanical necessity of integrity. This is not just a book about "doing better"; it is a guide to **repossessing your destiny**.

To the leaders who have felt their light flickering under the pressure of compromise, and to the mothers standing as gatekeepers over their children's potential: this is your mandate. It is time to move from the morning haze of uncertainty into the **Noon-Day Authority** of your assignment.

It is time to stay lit.

# DEDICATION

This work is dedicated first to **The Ancient of Days**, the Father of Lights, in whom there is no shadow of turning. You are the source of my luminosity and the Architect of my destiny.

**To my children and the generations yet unborn:** You are the "Stars of Zion" that I have carried in the womb of intercession. This manual is your inheritance, a spiritual "GPS" to ensure that you never wander, never dim, and never lose your coordinate in the firmament of your calling. I have stood at the gate to ensure your light remains untampered with. May you shine seven times brighter than those who came before you.

**To the "Praying Mothers" and the "Watchmen" of this age:** To those who refuse to let their lamps go out in the night. To the lionesses who roar over their cubs and the governors who refuse to vacate their seats at the gate. This is for you. May these decrees be the gavel in your hand that shatters every legal claim of the enemy over your household.

And finally, to the memory of **The Matriarchs and Patriarchs** of my bloodline who preserved the "flicker" of faith through the storms, until it could become the "White Fire" it is today. We are the fulfillment of your prayers.

**The night must bow, and the Star must Shine.**

# Table of Contents

# INTRODUCTION

In the archives of the Spirit, your existence is not a coincidence, nor is it a mere biological event. You were drafted into the firmament of time as a **Legislative Entity**. According to the Constitutional Decree of Genesis 1:16, you were appointed to be a "Lesser Light", a Star, commissioned to exercise *Mashal* (Dominion) over the night.

However, we find ourselves in an era where many "Stars of Zion" are flickering in obscurity. We see brilliant destinies muffled by "Marine Fogs" of confusion, "Cloudy Foundations" of ancestral iniquity, and the predatory tracking of "Herod spirits" who specialize in extinguishing great lights before they reach their noon day strength. Many believers are working hard but shining little, because their "Luminosity Quotient" has been siphoned by the thieves of the night.

**The Preservation of Stars** is a judicial response to this spiritual crisis.

This is not a book of religious theories; it is a **Manual of Governance.** It is based on a simple, immutable Kingdom Law: **Light does not argue with darkness; it displaces it.** If the darkness is prevailing in your industry, your health, or your household, it is not because the darkness is "strong", it is because the Star is not legally installed or properly polished.

Throughout these pages, we will conduct a thorough **Risk Assessment** of your destiny. We will identify the "Thieves of Luminosity" and provide the **Sanitization Protocols** to scrub the "Smog of Compromise" from your spiritual lens. We will navigate through this book with the protocol of:

**Recovery:** Finding the scattered fragments of your virtue.

**Alignment:** Fixing your star in its correct Prophetic Rank.

**Purification:** Polishing your light for high frequency impact.

**Activation:** Locking your seat at the Gate of the City.

Whether you are a mother guarding the "Seed Bank" of your children's future, or a marketplace leader seeking to navigate a dark economy, this manual will provide you with the **Judicial Compass** you need.

The night is no longer a place of fear for the one who knows their rank. It is merely the canvas upon which your glory is highlighted. It is time to stop apologizing for your brightness and start enforcing your rule.

**The Gavel has fallen. The Court is in session. Arise and Shine.**

# Chapter 1: The Anatomy of a Kingdom Star

## A. The Constitutional Definition: Celestial Governors

To understand your destiny, you must first understand the Judicial Language of the Creation Act. In the Kingdom, a star is not a "random decoration" in the sky; it is a **Legal Appointment**. When the Creator drafted the "Constitution of the Firmament," He established a hierarchy of light that serves as the blueprint for every believer's impact on earth.

### The Genesis 1:16 Statute: The Appointment of Rule

"And God made two great lights; the greater light to rule the day, and the lesser light to rule the night: he made the stars also." (Genesis 1:16)

In this verse, the Holy Spirit uses the word **"Rule."** This is the Hebrew word *mashal*, which means to have **Dominion, to Govern, or to Reign. The Star as a "Lesser Governor":** While the "Sun" (The Christ) rules the Day, the "Stars" (The Believers) are commissioned to Govern the Night. **Supporting Scripture:** *"Ye are the light of the world. A city that is set on an hill cannot be hid." (Matthew 5:14)*

You have a specific "Zone of Influence." Your "Shine" is the exercise of authority over the darkness in your specific industry, family, or territory.

The Scripture says *1 Corinthians 15:41 "There is one glory of the sun, and another glory of the moon, and another glory of the stars: for one star different from another star in glory."*

In the Constitutional hierarchy of Genesis 1:16, the Sun (the Greater Light) represents the manifest presence of Christ, the source of all light. However, the "Night" (the world system, the times of crisis, and spiritual blindness) is legally assigned to the Stars.

**The Commission:** You are not just a "believer"; you are a **Commissioned Governor**. When the world enters a "Night Season" (economic collapse, family trauma, or moral darkness), the Sun isn't physically visible, but the Stars are.

**The Responsibility:** Your job is not to complain about the darkness, but to **Govern** it. Darkness only expands where a "Star" refuses to exercise its (dominion).

**Matthew 5:14 (The Hilltop Statute):** A city on a hill cannot be hidden because its altitude combined with its light makes it a **point of reference**. As a Kingdom Star, you are set on the "Hill" of your specific calling to ensure the darkness has a boundary.

## Celestial Jurisdiction: Zones of Influence

In the physical universe, stars do not wander aimlessly; they are locked into specific coordinates. In the Kingdom, this is your **Jurisdiction**.

**The Industry Gate:** Your "Shine" is not meant to be generic. If you are in medicine, that is your **Celestial Zone**. You are authorized to legislate health and life in that "Night" sector. If you are in business, you are the Governor of that marketplace.

**Territorial Authority:** Your authority is highest within your specific assignment. A "Star" assigned to the family mountain cannot be eclipsed by the darkness of that lineage because they carry the **Executive Order** to rule that night.

**The "Zone" Protocol:** When you stay within your assigned jurisdiction, you carry the full backing of the Kingdom's "Military" (Angelic assistance).

## The Diversity of Glory (1 Corinthians 15:41)

*"For one star differeth from another star in glory."* This is the **Anti Comparison Clause**. It explains that while every believer is a star, every star has a different "Luminosity Quotient" and a different "Frequency of Impact."

**Different, Not Lesser:** One star may shine with the glory of *Wisdom* (Strategy), while another shines with the glory of *Power* (Healing/Miracles).

**The Constellation Effect:** You are not in competition with other believers. You are part of a **Prophetic Constellation**. When every star recognizes its unique glory and stays in its rank, the darkness is not just "managed" it is **defeated**.

**Specific Glory:** Your "Shine" is calibrated to the specific darkness you were born to conquer. Your "Glory" is actually your **Legal Weight** in the spirit realm.

As a Child of God "You are not an accident of biology; you are a **Statute of Genesis 1:16**. Your life is a **Celestial Jurisdiction**. When you enter a room, the 'Night' recognizes your rank. You aren't just there to exist; you are there to **Govern** the atmosphere by the weight of the Glory assigned to your name." Hebrews 10:7, which itself is drawing from Psalm 40: Then I said, Behold, I have come in the volume of the book it is written of me to do Your will, O God.

## B. The Star as a "Title Deed" of Destiny

In the archives of Heaven, your star serves as your **Prophetic Title Deed**. It is the celestial document that proves you have been granted "Right of Way" on the earth. It carries the data of your **"Luminosity Quotient"** the specific measure of the King's glory you are legally authorized to manifest in your generation.

## The Legislative Light: Voting vs. Vetoing

*"The light shineth in darkness; and the darkness comprehended it not." (John 1:5)*

In the Kingdom, light is not just a visual phenomenon; it is the highest form of **Legislation**.

**The "Vote" for Heaven:** When you shine through your gifts, your integrity, or your prayer, you are casting a "Legislative Vote" for the will of God to be done in that environment.

**The "Veto" of the Shadow:** Darkness is a "motion" filed by the enemy. When your star shines, you are **Vetoing** that motion. John 1:5 reveals that the darkness cannot "comprehend" (seize or overcome) the light. Legally, this means the darkness has no power of "Appeal" once the light has spoken. Your shine is your **Gavel**. Every time you manifest Kingdom excellence, you are striking the gavel and declaring, *"The darkness is overruled!"*

## The Fixed Position: The Judicial Seat

**Revelation 3:21** "To the one who is victorious, I will give the right to sit with me on my throne, just as I was victorious and sat down with my Father on his throne.

A star's power is tied to its **Position**. In astronomy, if a star leaves its orbit, it becomes a "falling star" or debris. In the spirit, if a believer abandons their "Judicial Seat," they lose their ability to legislate.

**The "Seat at the Gate":** In biblical times, the "Gate" was where the elders sat to make laws and judge cases. Your "Fixed Position" is your **Seat at the Gate** of your industry or family.

**The Risk of Falling:** A star "falls" when it chooses compromise over character or fear over faith. A fallen star is a Governor who has abandoned their post.

**Preservation:** Maintaining your star is about **Overcoming**. Revelation 3:21 links "overcoming" with "sitting on the throne." Your light remains a constant signal to the world only as long as you refuse to be displaced from your assigned Prophetic Seat.

## Judicial Decree:

"I strike the Gavel and I declare that my destiny is a **Title Deed** signed by the Blood of the Lamb! I invoke the **John 1:5 Statute** and I Veto every shadow trying to settle over my household! I refuse to be displaced; I refuse to fall; I refuse to vacate my Judicial Seat! I take my place at the Gate of my calling and I release the Legislative Light that cannot be overruled! My position is **Fixed**, my authority is **Final**, and my light is **Unstoppable**! In Jesus' Name!"

## C. The Navigation Protocol: Leading the Kings

The greatest function of a Kingdom Star is **Navigation**.

**The Bethlehem Standard:** When the "Star of the King" rose, it forced the "Kings of the Earth" to move. Scripture says, *Where is he that is born King of the Jews? for we have seen his star in the east, and are come to worship him." (Matthew 2:2)*

**The Impact of the Governor:** When you shine with the Spirit of Excellence, you are **Navigating** for others. Bible says; *"For, behold, the darkness shall cover the earth, and gross darkness the people: but the Lord shall arise upon thee, and his glory shall be seen upon thee. And the Gentiles shall come to thy light, and kings to the brightness of thy rising." (Isaiah 60:2-3)*

## The Navigation Protocol: Leading the Kings

The greatest function of a Kingdom Star is **Navigation**. You are not shining just to be admired; you are shining to provide a **Coordinate of Truth** in a world lost in the "Marine Fog" of deception.

### The Bethlehem Standard: Forcing the Move

*"Saying, Where is he that is born King of the Jews? for we have seen his star in the east and are come to worship him." (Matthew 2:2)*

The "Bethlehem Standard" establishes that a Kingdom Star has the power to **command the movement of secular authority.**

**The Signal to the Seekers:** The "Wise Men" were the intellectuals, the economists, and the political advisors of their day. They didn't move because of a sermon; they moved because they saw a **Celestial Signal**.

**Provoking the Journey:** When your star rises in your industry, it creates a "Holy Restlessness" in the kings of the earth. Your excellence and your results force them to leave their comfort zones and seek the source of your light.

**The Protocol:** You do not have to "chase" kings. If you maintain your luminosity, the kings are **spiritually obligated** to track your coordinate.

### The Impact of the Governor: The Spirit of Excellence

*"And the Gentiles shall come to thy light, and kings to the brightness of thy rising." (Isaiah 60:2-3)*

Navigation is not just about showing the way; it is about **Setting the Standard**. When you shine with the Spirit of Excellence, you are "Navigating" for others who are blind to the Kingdom way of doing things.

**Arising in Gross Darkness:** Isaiah 60 reveals that your light is most visible when "gross darkness" covers the people. Your ability to maintain peace in a crisis, integrity in a corrupt deal, and wisdom in a complex problem provides a **Judicial Compass** for others.

**The "Rising" Requirement:** The Gentiles and Kings come to the *brightness* of your rising. This means your visibility is proportional to your **Weight of Glory**.

**The Result:** You become a "City on a Hill" for your industry. People will look to your marriage, your business practices, and your leadership style to find their own way out of the darkness.

## The Navigato's Decree

"I strike the Gavel and I activate the **Navigation Protocol** over my life! I invoke the **Matthew 2:2 Bethlehem Standard**; I decree that my light is a signal that cannot be ignored by the leaders of my generation!

I reject the spirit of obscurity! I command the 'Kings of the East' to locate my coordinate and bring their resources to the feet of my King! I decree that as darkness covers the earth, my 'Luminosity Quotient' shall increase! I am a **Judicial Compass**; I am a **Celestial GPS**; I am a **Governor of Light**! I shall lead the kings to Zion, and they shall see the Glory of my Father upon me! In Jesus' Name!"

## The Spiritual Realty: Philippians 2:15

*"That ye may be blameless and harmless, the sons of God, without rebuke, in the midst of a crooked and perverse nation, among whom ye shine as lights in the world;" (Philippians 2:15)*

**The "Midst of Crookedness" Clause:** The darker the generation, the more **Essential** the star's shine becomes. Bible says; *"The path of the just is as the shining light, that shineth brighter and brighter unto the perfect day." (Proverbs 4:18)*

**The "Without Fault" Standard:** Integrity is the "Glass" through which your star shines. If the glass is dirty (compromise), the light is trapped. Bible says; *"The spirit of man is the candle of the Lord, searching all the inward parts of the belly." (Proverbs 20:27)*

## A Watchman's "Celestial Governance" Decree

"I strike the Gavel and I authorize the **Genesis 1:16 Mandate** over my life and my seed! I decree that we are NOT 'flickering candles', we are Celestial Governors appointed to rule the night!

I 'Veto' every attempt of the darkness to claim jurisdiction over our territory! I invoke the **Psalm 147:4 Statute**, He calls the stars by name and I decree that my star is 'Fixed and Functioning' in its Prophetic Rank!

I invoke the **Matthew 2:2 Bethlehem Standard** and I decree that our light shall force the 'Kings of the East' to bring their treasures to the feet of our Lord! I command the 'Lens of my Destiny' to be purged of all filth and compromise according to **Psalm 51:10**!

I 'Seal' my position in the firmament of the Kingdom! I shall not fall, I shall not dim, and I shall not be displaced! My light is a 'Judicial Signal' that provides navigation to my generation! We are the **Stars of Zion**! We carry the **Title Deed of Glory**! The night must bow, the fog must scatter, and the Star must Shine! In Jesus' Name!"

So , now its time to warfare for your star on this very Chapter One;

## Warfare prayer for chapter one: The Search and Seizure Mandate.

This is a **Judicial Counter Strike**. If the enemy has "pushed the envelope" by tampering with the Celestial Assets of a Child of God, then the response must be **Violent Legislation**. We are not asking; we are **Enforcing**.

We are moving from "Search" to **"Tactical Retrieval."** We are treating the star thief not as a neighbor, but as a **Criminal Insurgent** in the Kingdom Estate.

**Focus:** Locating the star and arresting the "Star Hunters."

**Scripture:** "The light shines in the darkness, and the darkness has not overcome it." John 1:5

## Category A: Arresting The Star Hunter (The "Herod" Strike)

Targeting the entities that track your rising to terminate it.

1. I strike the Gavel and invoke **Psalm 35:4-6**: Let every "Herod" spirit tracking my star be confounded and put to shame; let them be as chaff before the wind, and let the Angel of the Lord chase them!
2. I release the **Blindness of Elisha** (2 Kings 6:18) upon every monitoring entity and star gazer using demonic telescopes to track my destiny!
3. I decree a **Judicial Execution** of every "Star Hunter" that has vowed that my light will not reach its noon day; let their own pits swallow them!
4. By the power of **Psalm 7:15-16**, I command the mischief of the star thief to return upon his own head and his violent dealing to come down on his own crown!
5. I authorize a **Divine Ambush** against every coven and marine coven where my star is being discussed; let the Fire of God scatter their assembly!
6. I invoke the **Statute of Pharaoh's End** (Exodus 14); let the "Chariots" of my pursuers be jammed in the mud of their own wickedness!

## Category B: Breaking The Dark Vaults (Search & Rescue)

Locating the star in the archives of the deep.

7. I command the **Gates of Brass** to be broken and the **Bars of Iron** to be cut asunder (Isaiah 45:2); release my star from the "Treasure Houses of Darkness" now!
8. I invoke **Job 20:15**: The thief has swallowed my glory, but he shall vomit it up again; God shall cast it out of his belly by Fire!
9. I command the **Marine Wardens** holding my star in the "Watery Vaults" to be paralyzed by the Thunder of God's Voice (Psalm 29:3)!
10. I release the **Blood Scented Bloodhounds of Heaven** to track my star to the 127 provinces of the kingdom of darkness and bring it back!
11. I command every "Evil Pot" or "Jar of Limitation" holding my light to **Shatter** by the Hammer of the Lord (Jeremiah 23:29)!
12. I invoke **Jeremiah 51:44**: I will punish Bel in Babylon and make him spew out what he has swallowed! I command the "Bel" of my bloodline to vomit my star!

## Category C: Recovering The Star From The Hands Of The Thief

Severing the illegal possession.

13. I strike the hands of the star thief with the **Sword of the Spirit**; let his grip be broken and my star released instantly!
14. I invoke **Psalm 18:14**: I shoot out the Arrows of the Lord and scatter the star syndicate; I shoot out lightnings and discomfort them!
15. I declare that my star is **Lethal Cargo**; I command the fire of Hebrews12:29 to consume any demonic hand that refuses to let go of my light!
16. I revoke every **Illegal Bill of Sale** used to trade my star in the spirit realm; I wash the "Transaction Ledger" clean with the Blood of Jesus!
17. I command every "Altars of Exchange" where my star was swapped for a "Lesser Life" to be **Pulverized** by the East Wind of God!

18. I invoke **Zechariah 9:11-12**: By the Blood of the Covenant, I release the "Prisoners of Hope"! I command the "Waterless Pit" to release my star!

## Category D: Neutralizing The Effects Of Tampering

Stopping the damage in real time.

19. I command every "Demonic Veil" or "Black Bag" placed over my star to be **Incinerated** by the Fire of the Holy Ghost!
20. I break the "Curse of the Hidden Lamp" (Luke 8:16); I decree that the "Cover" is removed and my light is moving to the lampstand!
21. I command the "Siphons of the Night" to be disconnected from my soul; I recover every drop of "Virtue Oil" stolen from my lamp!
22. I invoke **Isaiah 49:25**: Even the captives of the mighty shall be taken away, and the prey of the terrible shall be delivered! I am DELIVERED!
23. I command the "Spiritual Magnetism" of the thief to be **Reversed**; let him now attract the judgments of God while I attract my glory!
24. I decree that every "Shadow of Death" cast over my star is dissolved by the **Sun of Righteousness** (Malachi 4:2)!
25. I strike the Gavel and conclude the Search: **The Thief is Caught, the Star is Found, and the Recovery is Total!**

## Declarations:

1. **The Sovereign Seal:** I decree that my life is no longer a "Public Domain" for siphons; I seal my estate under the **Standard of Holiness**, making it a Sovereign Kingdom territory.
2. **The Signal Lock:** I lock my spiritual frequency into the **Throne Room Connection**, ensuring that I am untraceable to trackers but highly visible to my "Open Reward."
3. **The Cargo Enforcement:** I declare that every "Missing Good" identified in my Divine Audit is now in transit; I refuse to settle for a partial delivery of my prophetic assets.
4. **The Veto Supremacy:** I exercise my final Veto over the "Smog of Compromise"; I will never again sign my virtue over to a system that requires the decay of my integrity.
5. **The Floor Decree:** I cement the "Star-Standard" for my lineage; I declare that the "Foundational Cracks" of my ancestors are permanently sealed by the Blood Covenant.
6. **The Soot Clearance:** I decree a total atmosphere clearance over my mind and business; every trace of "administrative soot" and "human overhead" is purged from my Star-Power.
7. **The Seed-Bank Security:** I declare my children's potential is **Constitutional Property**, guarded by a Legislative Hedge that no "Herod Spirit" can penetrate or bypass.
8. **The Momentum Mandate:** I annul every "Reset" cycle in my family history; from this moment forward, my house moves only from **Ceiling to higher Ceiling**.
9. **The Judicial Rest:** I occupy my "Seated Position" with absolute reliability; I refuse to flicker with anxiety, for I am anchored in the frequency of **Absolute Rest**.
10. **The Final Verdict:** I declare that my **Star Deliverance** is not a future hope but a present reality. I am a Fixed Star, my orbit is secured, and my light is unquenchable.

**IT IS WRITTEN. IT IS DECREED. IT IS DONE**

# Chapter 2: The Thieves of Luminosity

To preserve your star, you must conduct a **Judicial Risk Assessment**. In the spirit realm, your luminosity is a threat to the established darkness. As your brightness increases, you attract the attention of "Destiny Predators" whose sole mandate is to ensure your light never reaches its intended coordinate. Understanding these "thieves" is the first step in legislating their defeat.

## A. The "Herod" Entity: The Star Hunters

"Then Herod the Great, when he saw that he was mocked of the wise men, was exceeding wroth, and sent forth, and slew all the children that were in Bethlehem, and in all the coasts thereof, from two years old and under, according to the time which he had diligently enquired of the wise men." (Matthew 2:16)

The "Herod" Entity represents **Institutionalized Star Hunting**. This is a spirit that tracks the rising of a star before that star has even fully manifested its power.

**Tracking the Rising Star:** Just as the wise men saw a signal in the heavens, the enemy has "spiritual meteorologists" who track the sudden increase in a person's prayer life or prophetic rank. Bible says; *"Lest Satan should get an advantage of us: for we are not ignorant of his devices." (2 Corinthians 2:11)*

**Pre emptive Strike:** The Herod spirit does not wait for you to become a king; it tries to "kill the child" in the cradle. This manifests as sudden, unexplainable attacks on your health, reputation, or children the moment you move to a new level of Kingdom governance. This can start from pregnancy and follow the lineage. Attacks after attacks, bareness, premature death, unexplained loss. Young Stars are attacked as soon as they are conceived miscarriages, disorders, autism, Down syndrome, cerebral palsy, still birth.

**The Bible says;** "And his tail drew the third part of the stars of heaven, and did cast them to the earth: and the dragon stood before the woman which was ready to be delivered, for to devour her child as soon as it was born." *(Revelation 12:4)*

**The Legislative Response:** You must invoke the **Statute of Divine Misdirection**, making your star "invisible" to the radar of star hunters while remaining "luminous" to your destiny helpers. Bible says; *"For He shall hide me in His pavilion in the time of trouble; in the secret place of His tabernacle shall He hide me." (Psalm 27:5)*

## B. The Atmospheric Dampeners: Marine Fogs and Cloudy Foundations

If the enemy cannot kill the star, he attempts to **muffle the frequency** of its light. He uses "Atmospheric Dampeners" to create a spiritual environment where your shine is restricted.

**Marine Fogs:** This is the specialty of the marine kingdom, a "heaviness" or "confusion" that settles over your mind or household. It makes you feel "dim," uninspired, and tired, reducing your star to a "flickering candle" rather than a celestial governor. Bible says; "But their minds were blinded. For until this day the same veil remains uplifted in the reading of the Old Testament, because the veil is taken away in Christ." *(2 Corinthians 3:14)*

**Cloudy Foundations:** Unresolved iniquity or "cracked foundations" in your lineage create a "ceiling of clouds" over your life. Your light is absorbed by the cloud of the past, preventing it from reaching the "Marketplace." Closed heavens? *"If the foundations be destroyed, what can the righteous do?" (Psalm 11:3)*

**The Legislative Response:** You must use the **East Wind of God** to scatter the fog and the **Blood of Jesus** to sanitize the foundation, removing the "ceiling" between your light and your territory. Bible

Says; *"The east wind dried up her fruit: her strong rods were broken and withered; the fire consumed them." (Ezekiel 19:12)*

## B. The Smog of Compromise: The Film of Obscurity

While Herod attacks from the outside, the "Smog of Compromise" dims you from the **inside**. This is the most dangerous thief because it is "silent." It is dangerous because this is what had caused believers to be denied their right to be delivered because of this hidden silent sin.

**The Film of Compromise:** Every "small" hidden sin or moral shortcut creates a thin "film" over the lens of your star. Over time, these layers build up into a spiritual "smog." Bible says, *"A righteous man falling down before the wicked is as a troubled fountain, and a corrupt spring." (Proverbs 25:26)*

**Marketplace Invisibility:** In the spirit realm, visibility is tied to **Integrity**. When a star is covered in smog, it loses its Judicial Authority. You might work hard, but your "shine" is too weak to attract kings or resources. Bible says; *"The lamp of the body is the eye... if your eye is bad, your whole body will be full of darkness." (Matthew 6:22-23)*

**The Loss of Sharpness:** Compromise makes your light "blurry." You lose your edge and your ability to "Navigate" through complex business or family decisions. This makes it hard to reach your God given destiny. That is why many of our divine destinies are stunted in the Spirit.

Bible says;*"* Jesus said to them: "A little while longer the light is with you. Walk while you have the light, lest darkness overtake you; for he who walks in darkness does not know where he is going *(John 12:35)*

**The Legislative Response:** You must apply the **Standard of Blamelessness**. It is about keeping the "glass" of your star polished so the King's light passes through with 100% transparency.

**The Statute:** "that you may become blameless and harmless, children of God without fault in the midst of a crooked and perverse generation, among whom you shine as lights in the world," *(Philippians 2:15)*

## The Judicial Verdict

"I strike the Gavel and I release the 'Writ of Exposure' against every Thief of Luminosity! I invoke the **2 Corinthians 2:11 Statute**, I am not ignorant of your devices! I identify the Herod entity and I decree that his 'Search and Destroy' mission is **Vetoed**!

I command the Marine Fog and the Cloudy Foundations to scatter by the **East Wind of God** according to **Ezekiel 19:12**! I wash my foundation in the Blood of the Lamb!

I repent for every layer of the 'Smog of Compromise' I have allowed to settle on my star! I apply the **Philippians 2:15 Standard**; I polish my lens and I declare that the 'Film of Obscurity' is peeled off today! I am no longer invisible; I am no longer muffled! My star is sharp, my light is clean, and my frequency is **LETHAL** to the kingdom of darkness! In Jesus' Name!"

# Warfare prayer chapter two: The Re-Assembly & Alignment

Understood, Governor. We are removing the technical symbols and focusing on the raw, legislative power of the Word.

**Focus:** Gathering the "Scattered" pieces and fixing the star in its correct Prophetic Rank. **Scripture Anchor:** "He counts the number of the stars; He calls them all by name." Psalm 147:4

## Category A: The Great Gathering (The "Magnetic" Strike)

Forcing the return of every scattered fragment.

1. I strike the Gavel and invoke **Ezekiel 34:12**: As a shepherd seeks out his flock, I command the Holy Ghost to seek out every scattered fragment of my star and bring them back to my center!
2. I release a **Divine Magnetism** into the atmosphere; let every virtue stolen from my star by "star sponges" be pulled back to me by Fire!
3. I command the **Four Winds** (Ezekiel 37:9) to blow upon the valley of my scattered destiny and breathe life into every fragmented piece of my glory!
4. I invoke the **Statute of Total Retrieval** (1 Samuel 30:18-19): Nothing shall be lacking, small or great; I recover **ALL** that the "Amalekites" of the deep scattered!
5. I command every "Star Vampire" currently feeding on my light to **Vomit my Virtue** and perish by the Thunder of God (Job 20:15)!
6. I break the "Covenant of Fragmentation" that has made my life look like a "puzzle with missing pieces"; I receive my **Wholeness** now!

## Category B: Repairing The Celestial Structure (Suturing the DNA)

Fixing the cracks caused by trauma, sin, or generational leaks.

7. I use the **Blood of Jesus** to "Suture" every spiritual crack in my star; I decree that my light shall no longer leak into the abyss!
8. I invoke **Isaiah 58:12**: I am the "Repairer of the Breach" and the "Restorer of Streets to Dwell In"; I repair the structural integrity of my celestial identity!
9. I command every "Spiritual Parasite" living in the cracks of my soul to be **Flushed Out** by the Liquid Fire of the Holy Ghost!
10. I declare that my star is **One Single, Unbreakable Unit**; I reject the "Double Minded" frequency that scatters my power (James 1:8)!
11. I command the **Angels of Restoration** to weld the fragments of my star back together with the **Fire of the Altar**!
12. I invoke the **Law of the Finished Work**; what was broken in the first Adam is made **Perfectly Whole** in the Last Adam (1 Corinthians 15:45)!

## Category C: Positional Alignment (The "Prophetic Rank" Strike)

Moving the star from the "lowlands" to its "High Seat."

13. I strike the Gavel and command my star to **Exit** every "Low Orbit" of poverty and struggle; I move to the **Highest Frequency** of my calling!
14. I invoke **Psalm 75:6-7**: Promotion comes not from the east or west, but from God. I command my star to be **Elevated** to its legal Prophetic Rank!

15. I break every "Demonic Gravity" trying to pull my star down to the level of my ancestors' failures!
16. I command my star to be **Synchronized** with the "Clock of Zion"; I shall no longer be "Too Late" or "Too Early" for my breakthroughs!
17. I invoke the **Statute of Mordecai** (Esther 6): I command the "Kings of the Earth" to be restless until my star is honored and positioned in the Palace Gate!
18. I declare that my star is **Fixed and Unmovable**; I shall not be "Roused" from my seat of authority by any marine warden!
19. I command every "Replacement Star" or "Shadow Entity" masquerading in my position to be **Evicted and Executed**!

## Category D: Enforcing The Dominion Of The Light

Securing the gathered star against future scattering.

20. I invoke **Psalm 147:4**: If God calls the stars by name, then my star has a **Name of Power**. I activate that name to silence every storm!
21. I command a **"Fire Wall"** to be built around my gathered star; let it be an "Island of Light" that the deep cannot touch!
22. I break the "Spirit of the Nomad" (Genesis 4:12); I shall no longer wander in the spirit, but I shall **Occupy and Rule**!
23. I command my star to produce a **Frequency of Terror** to the kingdom of darkness and a **Frequency of Favor** to the sons of men!
24. I invoke the **Statute of Joshua's Sun** (Joshua 10:12-13): I command my star to **Stand Still** in its place of victory until the battle is won!
25. I strike the Gavel and decree: **My Star is Gathered, My Light is One, My Rank is Secured!**

## Declarations:

1. **I Disconnect The Taps:** I decree the immediate disconnection of every unauthorized "energy tap" where

human or spiritual systems have been feeding off my Star-Power without a Kingdom contract.

2. **I Annihilate The Mufflers:** I command every "Muffling Frequency" designed to suppress my voice and cloud my professional signal to be shattered by the sound of my Prophetic Rank.
3. **I Block The Illumination Theft:** I forbid any "Tracking System" from mapping the source of my innovation; my ideas are encrypted in the **Frequency of Silence** and are untouchable by the "Consumer."
4. **I Reject The Counterfeit Glow:** I Veto every temptation to trade my authentic "Fixed Star" light for the artificial, temporary "fame" offered by toxic social or corporate swarms.
5. **I seal The Radiance Leaks:** I authorize a total repair of my "Foundational Cracks," stopping the drainage of my virtue into the "Night Season" through compromise or people-pleasing.
6. **I Evict The Shadow Attachments:** I decree a legal separation from "Suicidal Attachments" and individuals whose only purpose is to cast a shadow over my brightness to hide their own mediocrity.
7. **I Purge The Soot of Envy:** I command the "Soot" of professional jealousy and the "Swarm" of competitive malice to be burned off my reputation by the fire of the Standard of Holiness.
8. **I Protect The Core Glow:** I declare that my internal joy, the fuel for my luminosity, is **Sovereign Cargo** and is legally protected from the "Chewing Locust" of daily stress.
9. **I Reclaim My Visibility:** I rescind every "Marine Fog" sent to make me invisible to my divine connections and financial partners; my light is now calibrated for **Maximum Impact.**
10. **I Lock The Luminosity:** I decree that my "Star" shall never experience a "Brownout" or a "Reset"; I am permanently locked into a frequency of increasing brilliance that no "Thief" can diminish.

**THE VERDICT:** The thieves are identified, their access is denied, and your light is restored to its maximum wattage. **Your Star is now untouchable.**

## Chapter 3: the Judicial Preservation of the Star

Recovery is a one time event, but Preservation is a daily legislative duty. In the spirit realm, an unprotected light is a target. To ensure your star remains "Fixed and Functioning," you must implement the Security Protocols of Zion. This chapter outlines the three primary layers of defense required to keep your luminosity at its peak and your coordinate secure.

**A. The "Shield of Glory": The Blood Sanitization** The atmosphere of this world is "corrosive" to spiritual light. Just as salt air corrodes metal, the "spirit of the age" seeks to dull the radiance of a Kingdom Governor.

**The Sanitization Protocol: The Biological Weaponry of the Spirit** You must use the Blood of the Lamb not just for the forgiveness of sins, but as a Sanitizing Agent. In a world currently under "Systemic Decay," the air is thick with the debris of other people's compromises. This spiritual smog attempts to settle on your visionary capacity, creating a layer of "ancestral soot" that dims your ability to see the next coordinate. The Blood acts as a high frequency solvent. When applied legislatively, it creates a "Glow Shield" an active, pulsing perimeter that neutralizes demonic pollutants upon contact. You are not just clean; you are "Bio demonically Secure."

**The Power of the Kavod: The Physics of Weighty Glory** When your atmosphere is "sanitized," the *Kavod* (the Weighty Glory) of God forms a protective hedge. This is not a thin, fragile veil; it is a dense, heavy presence. In the natural world, a star is a ball of gas held together by its own gravity and immense heat. Spiritually, the *Kavod* provides that internal pressure. It makes your star "too hot for scavengers to touch." Scavengers, those spirits that feed on the dimming lights of compromised leaders, cannot withstand the radiation of a sanitized atmosphere. As Psalm 3:3 declares, the Lord is not just a shield *around* you, but the *glory within* you that "lifts your head," positioning your star above the reach of the smog.

**Legislative Action: The Order of Sprinkling** To move from theory to governance; you must engage in the Legislative Action of sprinkling. This is the intentional, verbal application of the Blood over the specific "sectors" of your estate. You sprinkle the Blood over your **reputation**, ensuring that the "corrosive lies" of the enemy cannot stick to your name. You sprinkle it over your **finances**, creating a barrier against the "devourer" that targets the resources intended for your lineage. Finally, you sprinkle it over your **children's destinies**, ensuring their "Seed Bank" is kept in a sterile, heavenly environment. You are essentially "vaccinating" your future against the infections of the current age.

**The Maintenance of the Frequency** Preservation requires a daily audit of your "Luminous Output." If you feel your joy or clarity beginning to dim, it is a sign of "Atmospheric Encroachment." The spirit of the age has found a surface to settle on. Daily sanitization ensures that the "Fixed Star" of your leadership never develops a "blind spot." By maintaining a high frequency Shield of Glory, you ensure that your coordinate remains visible to those you are called to lead, and invisible to those who seek to extinguish you.

## B. The Statute of Non-Interference: The "No-Fly Zone"

In modern warfare, a "No-Fly Zone" is a legislated area where unauthorized aircraft are shot down upon entry. In the spirit, you must declare the same over your destiny. This is not a defensive prayer of "hope," but a judicial decree of territorial sovereignty.

### Blocking the Tracking: Neutralizing the Demonic Telescope

Monitoring spirits and "Star Gazers" operate as spiritual intelligence officers. They use "demonic telescopes" which manifest as psychic monitoring, toxic gossip, and familiar spirits to track the trajectory of your light. They are not just watching where you are; they are calculating where you are *going* so they can plant landmines in your future.

**The Frequency of Gossip:** Gossip is more than idle words; it is a spiritual sonar used to "ping" your location. When people speak against you, they are attempting to create a "frequency match" that allows monitoring spirits to lock onto your coordinate.

**Neutralizing the Signal:** To block the tracking, you must dismantle the "illegal spiritual mergers" that give these spirits a signal to follow. By sanitizing your environment, you create "Spiritual Stealth Technology," making your movements undetectable to those who seek to hinder your rising.

## The Mandate of Invisibility: The Secret Place Protocol

By invoking the Statute of Non Interference, you are issuing a legal notice to the kingdom of darkness: "You have no legal right to monitor my frequency." You are moving your star into the "Secret Place" of the Most High.

**The Shadow of the Almighty:** As Psalm 91:1 declares, the "Secret Place" is a realm of divine encryption. When you abide under the "Shadow of the Almighty," you are not just safe; you are **invisible**. A shadow is a region where light is blocked; in this context, the glory of God acts as a "Dark Matter" shield that prevents the enemy's light sensors from detecting your star.

**The Frequency Shift:** Invisibility occurs when you shift your frequency out of the reach of "Systemic Decay." You are still present in the marketplace and the industry, but your "Navigational Governance" is being directed from a private channel that the enemy cannot hack.

## Legislative Action: The Writ of Non Interference

Governance requires the active issuance of a "Writ of Non Interference." This is a formal judicial decree that forbids the enemy from siphoning your virtue or projecting shadows into your orbit.

**Decreeing Judicial Blindness:** You must command "Judicial Blindness" upon every "Herod" (leaders or spirits threatened by your rising) who is tracking your movements. Just as the angels struck the men at Lot's door with blindness, you decree that the "Star-Gazers" lose their ability to perceive your strategic moves.

**Enforcing the Orbit:** You are legislating that your orbit is a "Restricted Airspace." Any projection be it a "mother's warning" of fear, a cultural curse, or a professional sabotage is intercepted by the "Shield of Glory" before it can settle.

**The Virtue Lock:** Siphoning happens when the enemy finds a "leak" in your character. The Writ of Non Interference "seals the vessel," ensuring that the virtue required for your "Noon Day" authority remains within your "Kingdom Estate."

**The Decree:** "By the authority of the Standard of Holiness, I legislate a No-Fly Zone over my destiny. I invoke the Statute of Non-Interference against every monitoring spirit. I move my frequency into the Secret Place, and I decree that every eye tracking my star is struck with judicial blindness. My trajectory is encrypted in the Kavod, and my virtue is secure."

## C. Cleaning the Lens: The Role of Purity and Integrity

In the mechanics of celestial governance, the quality of the light is only as effective as the clarity of the medium through which it travels. You can possess a "Noon Day" destiny, but if the "glass" of your character is obscured, the world will only see a distorted shadow of your potential. Integrity is the "Optical Grade" of your star, it determines the precision and reach of your influence.

## The High Frequency Requirement: Purity as Mechanical Necessity

In Kingdom governance, purity is often taught as a moral suggestion, but in the realm of spiritual physics, it is a **Mechanical Necessity**. High frequency luminosity the kind required to rule a "dark" industry requires a clear path.

**The Film of Grease:** Compromise, whether it manifests as "gray areas" in business, double mindedness in decision making, or hidden "sexual altars," creates a spiritual film of grease on the lens of your soul.

**Scattered Light vs. Piercing Light:** When light hits a greasy lens, it scatters. Instead of a laser focused "Coordinate of Truth" that provides direction, your leadership becomes a blurry, weak glow that cannot pierce through the "cultural fog." To maintain a high frequency shine, you must eliminate the debris of compromise that causes your spiritual signal to dissipate.

## The Polishing Effect: Transparency for the King's Light

A life of integrity acts as a constant "Polishing Agent." It ensures that there is no "refractive error" in your character. When the lens of your soul is transparent, 100% of the King's light passes through you into the marketplace without being filtered by your ego or your appetites.

**The Sight of God:** As Matthew 5:8 declares, *"Blessed are the pure in heart: for they shall see God."* On a judicial level, this means that your "vision" is unobstructed. Because you see God clearly, you see your industry, your family, and your enemies clearly.

**Reflective Governance:** By extension, when you are polished, the world sees God *through* you. You become a "Legislative Mirror" that reflects the Standard of Holiness into environments that have forgotten what purity looks like.

## Legislative Action: The Lens Check and the Single Eye

Governance requires a daily "Lens Check." Just as a precision instrument must be calibrated, the Kingdom Governor must proactively remove the "film" of the day.

**Rapid Repentance:** Repentance is not just a prayer for forgiveness; it is a "Cleaning Protocol." It is the act of wiping away the day's soot so that it doesn't bake onto the lens.

**The Single Eye (Matthew 6:22):** You must maintain a "Single Eye" a singular focus on Kingdom standards. When your vision is divided between Kingdom principles and worldly shortcuts, your "body of work" becomes dark. A "Single Eye" ensures that your entire estate remains flooded with light, leaving no dark corners for "monitoring spirits" to hide in.

## The Preservation Decree: Breaking Down the Power

This decree is not a request; it is a **Judicial Activation**. When you speak these words, you are moving the "Gavel of Heaven" into your personal atmosphere.

**"I strike the Gavel and I activate the Shield of Glory":** You are initiating a legal proceeding. You are announcing that the "Security Protocols of Zion" are now live over your life.

**"Soaking the atmosphere in the Blood... Sanitized and Secure":** You are applying the "Bio demonic" vaccine. You are making your environment toxic to the "scavengers" of the night.

**"I legislate a No-Fly Zone... I decree Judicial Blindness":** You are blind siding the "Star Gazers." You are essentially "jamming the radar" of the enemy so they can no longer track your strategic movements.

**"I am hidden in the Secret Place":** You are invoking the Psalm 91:1 Statute of encryption. You are moving into a realm where the enemy's weapons cannot find a target.

**"I command the 'Lens of my Heart' to be polished":** You are taking responsibility for your frequency. You are rejecting the "smog of compromise" and choosing the "High Frequency Shine" that makes you a Governor of Light.

This decree establishes you as a **Fixed Star**. It moves you from a "victim" who is being hunted to a "Governor" who is being hidden in plain sight. It ensures that while you are visible enough to lead, you are too "sanitized" to be touched and too "polished" to be dimmed. You are enforcing the **Standard of Holiness** as a permanent law over your bloodline.

## Warfare Prayers Chapter Three: The Purification & Polishing of the Star.

On **Day 3**, we are moving into the **Sanitization Phase**. In the spirit, darkness doesn't just attack; it "clings." The enemy uses "Demonic Smog" and "Marine Moisture" to create a film of obscurity over your life, making you invisible to your helpers and unattractive to your opportunities.

You may have recovered your star (Chapter 1) and put it back together (Chapter 2), but if it is covered in the "Scent of the Deep" or the "Dust of Delay," it cannot radiate the **Kavod** (Weighty Glory) of the King. Today, we are not just praying; we are **Scrubbing**. We are using the Blood of the Lamb and the Fire of the Spirit to polish your destiny until it becomes a "Blinding Frequency" to every monitoring spirit.

**Focus:** Scrubbing the star of "Demonic Smog," "Marine Moisture," and the "Scent of the Deep." **Scripture Anchor:** "For look, the darkness shall cover the earth... but the Lord will arise over you, and His glory will be seen upon you." (Isaiah 60:2)

## Category A: Burning The Smog (The "Incineration" Strike)

Removing the layers of spiritual filth that dim your brightness.

1. I strike the Gavel and command the **Fire of God** (Hebrews 12:29) to burn off every layer of "Demonic Smog" and "Industrial Dust" that has settled on my star!
2. I wash my star in the **Blood of Jesus** to remove every "Scent of Death" and "Scent of the Marine Kingdom" attached to my identity!
3. I command the "Marine Moisture" of lust, perversion, and emotional instability to be **Dried Up** by the heat of the Sun of Righteousness (Malachi 4:2)!
4. I invoke the **Statute of Malachi 3:2-3**: I declare that the Lord is sitting as a **Refiner and Purifier** over my star, purging every ancestral dross!
5. I command every "Shadow of Obscurity" cast over my destiny by the "Mother of Harlots" to be **Dissolved** by the Light of Zion!
6. I break the "Curse of the Dimmed Lamp" over my bloodline; I scrub off the soot of failure and the grime of poverty!

## Category B: Purging The Lens (The "Transparency" Strike)

Cleaning the spiritual optics through which your glory shines.

7. I command every "Demonic Veil" or "Black Bag" placed over my star by monitoring spirits to be **Incinerated** now!
8. I use the "Hyssop of the Spirit" (Psalm 51:7) to purge my star of every secret compromise and hidden stain of the flesh!
9. I command the "Film of Disfavor" to be peeled off my life like a snake shedding skin; I receive the **Glittering Shine** of the Holy Ghost!
10. I break the "Spirit of the Gray Area"; I decree that my star is **Transparent and Pure**, reflecting the face of the King without distortion!
11. I command every "Cloud of Confusion" that has made my star appear dim to my helpers to be **Scattered** by the North Wind!
12. I strike every "Mirror of Vanity" used to distract my star; I decree that my focus is **Purified** and my light is **Sharp**!

## Category C: Removing The Marks (The "Sanitization" Strike)

Erasing the labels and marks of the enemy.

13. I command every "Mark of the Beast," "Mark of Shame," or "Label of Defeat" placed on my celestial identity to be **Blotted Out** by the Blood!
14. I command the "Siphons of the Night" to be disconnected; I recover every drop of **Anointing Oil** stolen from my star!
15. I invoke **Zechariah 3:3-4**: I command the "Filthy Garments" to be removed from my star, and I put on the **Festal Robes** of Glory!
16. I declare that my star is **Antiseptic** no demon or scavenger can touch my light without being burned by the Fire of God!
17. I command every "Salt Water Deposit" from the marine kingdom to be flushed out of my spirit by the **River of Life** (Revelation 22:1)!

18. I break the "Jar of Limitation" that has kept my light in a confined space; I decree a **Global Expansion** of my shine!

## Category D: Radiating The Glory (The "Brilliance" Strike)

Activating the high-frequency shine of the Governor.

19. I command my **Luminosity Quotient** to increase by seven times, even as the furnace of Nebuchadnezzar was heated seven times!
20. I invoke **Isaiah 60:1**: I command my star to "Arise and Shine," for my light has come and the **Glory of the Lord** is risen upon me!
21. I command the **Oil of Joy** (Psalm 45:7) to be the fuel that keeps my star burning with an unquenchable flame!
22. I declare that my star is now a **Reflector of the Kavod**; the weighty presence of God is the "Polish" on my life!
23. I command my star to "Pierce" through every dark situation, providing **Sudden Clarity** to my family and industry!
24. I decree that the "Rust of the Past" is gone; my star is **Fresh, New, and Blinding** to the kingdom of darkness!
25. I strike the Gavel and decree: **My Star is Purged, My Lens is Clear, My Shine is Sovereign!**

## Declarations:

1. **I Declare** that the "Beauty of the Lord" is the permanent finish upon my star!
2. **I Declare** that I am "Blameless and Harmless," shining as a star in a crooked generation (Philippians 2:15)!
3. **I Declare** that the "Smell of Fire" is my defense; no scavenger dares to approach my light!

4. **I Declare** that my "Prophetic Rank" is now visible and **Verified** by the Courts of Heaven!
5. **I Declare** that every "Stain of the Deep" is washed away; I am native to Zion!
6. **I Declare** that my "Excellence" is the fruit of my star's purity!
7. **I Declare** that I am **Visible for Victory** but **Invisible for Victimization**!
8. **I Declare** that the "Spirit of the Gray Area" is dead; my light is **Pure White Fire**!
9. **I Declare** that I have "20/20 Spiritual Vision" because my star is clean!
10. **I Declare** that **I AM PURGED, I AM POLISHED, AND I AM RADIANT!**

# Chapter 4: Navigational Governance (The Impact of Shining)

## A. The Star as a Compass: Leading the Lineage

In the same way the Star of Bethlehem provided a fixed, non-negotiable point of reference in the night sky, your personal integrity acts as the **North Star** for your family and organization. Leadership is not about shouting directions; it is about becoming a celestial marker that others can use to calculate their own position. **3 John 1:4 (KJV)** *"I have no greater joy than to hear that **my children walk in truth**."*

### The GPS of the Spirit

How your consistent walk provides a "Coordinate of Truth" for your children and employees who are lost in the cultural fog. In a "post truth" culture, values are often shifting and subjective this is the **cultural fog**. When a leader is inconsistent, those following them become "disoriented," much like a GPS losing its satellite signal.

**The Coordinate of Truth:** Consistency is your greatest asset. When your "yes" is always "yes" and your private life matches your public platform, you provide a fixed coordinate.

**Safety in the Fog:** When children or employees face moral ambiguity or professional crises, they don't look for a lecture; they look for a "steady signal." By maintaining your spiritual and ethical standards, you provide the data points they need to recalibrate their own lives and find their way back to solid ground.

### The Bethlehem Standard

When you shine, "Wise Men" (Resources and Helpers) are forced to move toward you. The Star of Bethlehem did not chase the Wise Men; it simply **occupied its place with such intensity** that those seeking the King had no choice but to follow its light. This is the law of spiritual attraction.

**The Magnetism of Excellence:** "Wise Men" represent high level resources, strategic partners, and divine helpers. These entities are not attracted to desperation; they are attracted to **clarity and light**.

**Forced Alignment:** When you establish a "Standard of Holiness" you create a vacuum that pulls in the right assets. Resources are "forced" to move toward you because your life represents a successful "Kingdom Estate." In the Kingdom economy, provision always follows the path of the light. If you want the resources of the "Wise Men," you must first provide the "Star" for them to follow.

## B. Stability and Excellence: The Wisdom of Transactions

In this second section, the focus shifts from the celestial "Star" to the grounded reality of the marketplace. Here, you define how spiritual authority translates into professional dominance through the concept of **Legislative Integrity**.

In the Kingdom, your work is your witness. This section explores how to maintain a high "Standard of Holiness" while operating in high stakes environments where compromise is the status quo.

### Practical Luminosity

Shining is not "shouting"; it is the Excellence of your execution. Most people associate "shining" with verbal proclamation. In the realm of governance, however, light is measured by **precision and reliability**. When your execution is flawless, it creates a "light" that others must acknowledge, even if they don't share your faith.

**Wisdom as Transparency:** In the dark, people rely on manipulation and "fine print." Divine Wisdom acts as a light that makes every transaction transparent. When you operate with total integrity, you eliminate the "hidden traps" that often cause business, projects,  deals to fail.

**The Prosperity of Trust:** Prosperity follows the path of least resistance. By being the most "stable" person in the room, you become the person everyone wants to transact with. Your excellence is the "Star" that guides resources to your estate.

**Proverbs 22:29** "Do you see a man who **excels in his work**? He will stand before kings; He will not stand before unknown men."

Excellence is the "Legislative Key" that unlocks the doors to the Palace. You don't beg for an audience with Kings; your "Standard of Excellence" forces the door open. It is the practical luminosity of a job well done that grants you governance.

## The Governance of the Night

How to rule a "dark" industry without being stained by its darkness? To govern the "night," you must realize that light is not "fighting" the dark,  it is simply occupying space. You can be at the top of a cutthroat industry without absorbing its "systemic decay."

**The Law of Non Porosity:** Just as a boat is in the water but is not supposed to let the water *into* it, a Kingdom leader is in the world but is "non porous" to its corruption. You rule by refusing to enter into "illegal spiritual mergers" or "ungodly soul ties" for the sake of a deal.

**Occupying the Void:** Darkness is simply the absence of light. When you bring the "Standard of Holiness" into a dark industry, you aren't just an employee or an owner, you are a **Governor**. You set the temperature and the rules of engagement for everyone within your sphere of influence.

Bible says**, Daniel 6:3** "Then this Daniel began distinguishing himself among the commissioners and satraps because **an extraordinary spirit was in him**, and the king planned to appoint him over the entire kingdom."

Daniel didn't survive Babylon by being loud; he ruled it because he was "extraordinary." His stability made him the only safe choice to lead. To rule the night, you must be the most "transparent" and "consistent" entity in the room, making you the only one capable of handling the King's business without corruption.

Bible says **, Proverbs 22:29** "Do you see a man who excels in his work? He will stand before kings; He will not stand before unknown men." This scripture is the legislative basis for the "Magnetic Standard." It does not say the man who *prays* more or *shouts* more will stand before kings, though prayer is the engine. It says the man who **excels in his work**.

Excellence is the passport to the Palace. In the Kingdom, "Kings" (high level decision makers and influencers) are looking for "Stability." They are tired of the "unknown men" who offer flickering promises and shoddy execution. When you excel, you are issuing a "Celestial Summons" to the gates of power. You are telling the systems of this world that you have the capacity to handle the weight of their highest transactions without breaking, because you are anchored in the **Standard of Holiness**.

## Legislative Action: The Marketplace Audit

**Examine the "Optical Grade" of your work:** Are there "hidden clauses" or shortcuts in your current projects?

**Polishing the Execution:** Identify one area of your professional life where you can move from "sufficient" to "excellent."

**The Declaration:** "I decree that my transactions are transparent and filled with the King's Wisdom. I reject the shortcuts of the night! I activate the Magnetic Standard of Excellence, and I command every 'Wise Man' assigned to my destiny to see my light and move toward my estate. I will not stand before unknown men; I stand before Kings! In Jesus' Name!"

## C. The "Daystar" Rising: From Flickering to Established

In this section, we move from the **activity** of the marketplace to the **authority** of a settled position. This is the transition from someone who is *striving* to someone who is *established.* Stability is the ultimate goal of Kingdom leadership. While many can achieve a temporary "glow" of success, the goal of this "Manual of Governance" is to turn your life into a permanent fixture in the spiritual and professional firmament.

### The Law of Increase

Moving from a "Flash in the Pan" to a "Fixed Star" that cannot be moved. In the digital and corporate age, many people are "flashes" sudden bursts of talent or success that disappear just as quickly because they lack a "Foundational" anchor.

**Dismantling the Flickering:** A "flicker" in your leadership is usually caused by an "ungodly soul tie" or a "hidden past" When these are dismantled, the power surge of your purpose no longer trips the breaker.

**The Fixed Star:** Once you are healed and aligned with the "Standard of Holiness," you become a fixed star. You are no longer "rattled" by industry shifts or cultural echoes. Your leadership becomes an immovable landmark that others use to find their way.

**Proverbs 4:18** “But the path of the just is as the shining light, that **shineth more and more** unto the perfect day."

This is the "Law of Increase." Your light is not designed to dim with age or market crashes. Because your path is "just" (legally aligned with Heaven), it is programmed for a steady, incremental increase in brightness and authority.

## The Perfect Day

Reaching the level of "Noon Day" authority where your influence is absolute. "The Perfect Day" is the spiritual equivalent of High Noon. At noon, the sun is directly overhead, and **shadows disappear. Shadowless Leadership:** When you reach this level of "Noon Day" authority, there is no "shadow of turning" in you. Your reputation is so established and your "Kingdom Estate" so secure that the "darkness" of the industry has no place to hide in your presence.

**Absolute Influence:** This isn't about control; it's about **weight**. At this stage, your words carry the force of a "Legislative Instrument." When you speak, the "Gavel falls" because your life has earned the right to issue a "celestial summons." You have moved from a victim of circumstances into a place of absolute authority.

**Job 11:17** "Life will be **brighter than noonday**, and darkness will become like morning."

This promises that your "governance" will reach a point where even your "darkest" moments have more light in them than a regular person's "morning." This is the result of repossessing what was stolen from your destiny and establishing a new bloodline standard.

This is the **Statute of Progression**. It reveals that for the "just", those legally aligned with the King, diminishing is not an option. If your light is fading, there is a judicial breach that needs to be addressed. The "Perfect Day" is your legal right. It is the state of being **Established**. While the world's leaders eventually burn out or are eclipsed by scandal, the Kingdom Governor is programmed for a "Daystar" rising that never ends.

**The Decree:** "I am a Daystar Rising! I reject the flicker of compromise and the short-circuit of double mindedness! By the Law of Increase, my light shines brighter and brighter every day. I am moving into my Noon Day Authority, where every shadow of my past is swallowed up in the Kavod! I have repossessed my destiny, I am Fixed, and I am Established as a shadowless leader in my generation! In Jesus' Name!"

## Warfare prayer, chapter four: The Installation & Activation of the Star.

On **Day 4**, we reach the **Legislative Zenith**. Recovery and purification are complete; now comes the **Installation**. In the spirit realm, a star that is not "Fixed" is a wandering star. Today, your destiny is moving into the **Highest Orbit** of your calling. You are moving from being a "candidate for glory" to being a **Sovereign Governor** of the light.

You are activating the **Navigational Power** of your star. From this day forward, your light will no longer just exist; it will **Command**. It will dictate the atmosphere of your home, your business, and your territory.

**Focus:** Locking the star into the "Seat at the Gate" and activating its "Navigational Power." **Scripture:** "Arise, shine; For your light has come! And the glory of the Lord is risen upon you." (Isaiah 60:1)

## Category A: The Celestial Bolt (The "Installation" Strike)

Locking your star into its legal Prophetic Seat.

1. I strike the Gavel and **Install** my star in the "Highest Orbit" of my calling; I command the Angels of Authority to bolt my destiny into its legal Prophetic Seat
2. I invoke the **Statute of Permanence** (Psalm 125:1); I decree that my star is like Mount Zion, which cannot be moved but abides forever
3. I command a **No-Fly Zone** over my destiny; I decree that no unauthorized entity or marine monitoring spirit can pass the borders of my light
4. I declare that my "Seat at the Gate" is occupied; I refuse to be a "Nomadic Star" wandering in search of identity
5. I invoke **Colossians 1:13**: I have been delivered from the power of darkness and **Translated** into the Kingdom of the Son; my star is now a permanent resident of the Third Heaven
6. I command the "Celestial Locks" of Zion to snap into place over my life; my position is **Non Negotiable** and **Non Transferable**!

## Category B: Activating The Bethlehem Signal (The "Navigational" Strike)

Forcing the world to respond to your rising.

7. I activate the **"Bethlehem Signal"** over my star; I command my destiny helpers to track the frequency of my light from the ends of the earth (Matthew 2:1-2)!

8. I invoke **Isaiah 60:3**: The Gentiles shall come to my light, and Kings to the brightness of my rising! I decree a **Magnetic Attraction** of resources to my feet!
9. I command my star to "Ignite" and stay burning **24/7**; I break every "Switch of Sabotage" used to turn off my influence in the marketplace!
10. I declare that my star is now a **Navigational Compass** for my generation; those who follow my light shall find the King!
11. I command the "Wealth of the Seas" and the "Treasures of the Darkness" to be diverted to my coordinate by the signal of my star!
12. I invoke the **Law of Occupancy**; wherever my light reaches, the Kingdom of God rules and every "Locust" must flee!

## Category C: The Sovereign Glow (The "Dominion" Strike)

Enforcing the rule of your light over the night.

13. I strike the Gavel and activate the **"Governor's Protocol"**; I rule the night through my luminosity, just as the stars were appointed in Genesis 1:16!
14. I command every "Sleeping Virtue" in my DNA to **Wake Up and Produce**; the season of "Potential" is over, the season of **Performance** is here!
15. I invoke **Psalm 110:2**: The Lord shall send the rod of your strength out of Zion. **Rule in the midst of your enemies!**
16. I declare that my "Shine" is an **Eviction Notice** to every spirit of infirmity, poverty, and delay in my household!
17. I command every "Herod" spirit to be struck with the **Angel of Judgment** at the news of my final activation (Acts 12:23)!
18. I break the "Limit of the Clouds"; I decree that my star has pierced the second heaven and is now drawing power

directly from the **Throne of Grace IN THE 3RD HEAVEN**!

## Category D: Sealing The Firmament (The "Security" Strike)

Ensuring the light / Star can never be tampered with again.

19. I use the **Blood of Jesus** to "Seal" the atmosphere around my star; I decree a permanent barrier against star hunters and star sponges!
20. I invoke **Psalm 121:6**: The sun shall not strike me by day, nor the moon by night. My light is **Shielded** from celestial and terrestrial attacks!
21. I command my star to be "Inter locked" with the **Lion of Judah**; I am a part of the "Great Constellation of the King"!
22. I declare that my voice now carries the **Frequency of the Roar**; when I speak, the light intensifies and the enemy retreats!
23. I command the **North Wind** to carry the news of my "Rising" to every boardroom of power where my name must be mentioned! Broadcasting Angel Broadcast my name now.
24. I declare that I am **Heavily Guarded** by Chariots of Fire; my star is the most "Highly Protected Asset" in this territory!
25. I strike the Gavel and decree: **my star is activated, my seat is secured, and my dominion is absolute!**

## Declarations:

1. **I Declare** that my "Morning" has finally arrived; the long night of obscurity is **Vetoed**!
2. **I Declare** that I am the **Head and Not the Tail**, for my star has been installed at the top of the firmament!
3. **I Declare** that I am **Positional and Operational**; I am in the right place, doing the right thing, at the right time!
4. **I Declare** that my star is a "Burning and a Shining Light" that cannot be hidden or extinguished!
5. **I Declare** that I am **Occupying the Gate** of my industry through the power of my restored luminosity!
6. **I Declare** that my "Star-Power" is dedicated to the **Exaltation of Jesus Christ**!
7. **I Declare** that I shall not be "Roused" or "Disturbed" from my seat of rest ever again!
8. **I Declare** that the "Price of the Blood" has made my activation **Irreversible**!
9. **I Declare** that my "Prophetic Title Deed" is now **Vindicated and Visible** to all!
10. **I Declare** that **I AM RISEN, I AM SHINING, AND I AM DOMINATING!**

# Chapter 5: The Mother of Lions as a Star Protector

## The Guardianship of the Lineage

The identity of a mother in the Kingdom is far more significant than biological nurturance; she is a celestial gatekeeper and a strategic protector of destinies. In this chapter, we move from the general governance of an industry into the specific, fierce guardianship of the bloodline. While scripture often refers to children as arrows in a quiver, there is a deeper, atmospheric reality at play.

## The Quiver of Stars: Catching and Positioning

Viewing your children not just as arrows, but as "Falling Stars" that have been "Caught and Positioned" by the Mother's Altar. In a world that seeks to darken the brightness of the next generation before they ever find their orbit, the Mother of Lions stands as the one who catches "Falling Stars." Many children enter the world with high velocity destinies, but without the spiritual atmosphere of a mother's altar, they risk burning out upon entry into a toxic culture.

### The Atmospheric Shield: Intercepting the Fall

You are not merely raising children; you are catching divine light and positioning it within a secure framework of holiness. In the natural world, a falling star (a meteor) burns up because of the friction of the atmosphere it enters. Similarly, the "spirit of the age" is a friction filled atmosphere designed to incinerate the destiny of your children before they ever find their purpose.

**The Legislative Interception:** You use your spiritual authority to intercept the "fall." The fall represents the mistakes of the past, the gravitational pull of generational curses, and the cultural traps laid by a system of decay. As a Mother of Lions, you create a "Sanitized

Atmosphere" around your home. This shield absorbs the friction so your children don't have to.

**Neutralizing the Heat:** Your standard of holiness acts as a cooling agent. While other children are being consumed by the "heat" of societal pressure and "sexual altars," your children are protected because you have legislated a "No Fly Zone" over their developing spirits.

### The Altar as a Landing Strip: The Secret Place Incubation

You hold that seed in the secret place of the Most High until it is ready to be released as a fixed coordinate in the earth. Your prayer life is the legislative instrument that ensures they don't "crash land" into the world's systems but are positioned for maximum impact.

**Controlled Entry:** A landing strip is a place of prepared arrival. By maintaining a consistent altar, you are preparing the ground for their destiny to manifest safely. You are not just hoping they turn out well; you are engineering their entry into adulthood.

**Strategic Release:** A star that is "caught" must eventually be "positioned." Your altar is the place where you receive the "Coordinate of Truth" for each child. You aren't just pushing them into a career; you are releasing them into a specific, divine orbit where their light will be most effective.

Bible says in, **Psalm 113:9** *"He grants the barren woman a home, Like a joyful mother of children." (In the original Hebrew context, this suggests a woman who is "established" as the pillar of the household.)*

Bible says in , **Revelation 12:1,** *"Now a great sign appeared in heaven: a woman clothed with the sun... and the dragon stood before the woman who was ready to give birth, to devour her Child as soon as it was born."*

This passage in Revelation reveals the "Mother of Lions" in her full celestial context. The "Woman clothed with the sun" is the ultimate Star Protector. Notice that the enemy (the dragon) is not waiting for the child to grow up; he is positioned at the moment of birth to "siphon" the light immediately.

As a Mother of Lions, you recognize that the attack on your children is **preemptive**. The enemy knows the "velocity" of their star. Therefore, your "Atmospheric Shield" must be active before they are even born, and your "Altar as a Landing Strip" must be lit 24/7. You are the woman clothed with the sun, you are so filled with the King's light that you become the primary defense against the devouring spirits of your generation.

## Legislative Action: The Lineage Decree

**Sanitizing the Atmosphere:** Use the "Order of Sprinkling the Blood of Jesus" over your children's rooms, their schools, and their digital devices.

**Positioning the Seed:** Call your children by their Kingdom assignments, not just their names.

**The Declaration:** "I strike the Gavel and I declare that my children are a Quiver of Stars! I catch every falling trajectory in my bloodline and I position it upon the Altar of the Most High! I enforce an Atmospheric Shield over their destinies; no demonic friction shall burn them! I reject the crash landing of compromise! My children shall not be siphoned; they are Fixed Stars, caught by a Mother's Altar and released into Noon Day Authority! In Jesus' Name!"

## B. Guarding the Seed Bank's Light: Preventing the Siphon

Every child enters this world as a high value target. They carry within them a **"Seed Bank"** a multi-generational repository of divine potential, genetic strength, and specific spiritual assignments. The adversary is indifferent to your children's comfort or happiness; his objective is strictly "extractive." He seeks to **siphon** their light while it is still in its vulnerable morning phase, ensuring they never reach the absolute authority of their **Noon Day**.

### Identifying the Siphon: The Theft of Innocence

Siphoning is a quiet, steady drainage of spiritual virtue. It does not always happen through overt tragedy; it often occurs through **premature exposure**. When a child is exposed to images, spirits, or "sexual altars" before they have the spiritual skeletal structure to process them, a leak is created in their Seed Bank.

**Illegal Spiritual Mergers:** These are the soul ties and "unauthorized covenants" formed in youth often through the digital gateways of the "cultural fog." These mergers create a pipeline where the **child's virtue is siphoned out** and the "**systemic decay" of the world is pumped in.**

### The Mechanics of the Siphon: Illegal Spiritual Mergers

In the architecture of the spirit, a "merger" is the joining of two entities to share resources, identity, and destiny. While God ordained the "Covenant" as a merger of life and blessing, the enemy utilizes **Illegal Spiritual Mergers** to create unauthorized pipelines into the next generation. These are soul ties and "shadow covenants" formed in the vulnerability of youth, often facilitated by the "digital gateways" of the cultural fog.

**The Pipeline of Exchange:** An illegal merger acts as a two way conduit. It is not merely a "bad influence"; it is a functional plumbing system in the spirit realm.

**The Virtue Outflow:** Through these mergers, formed through premature sexual exposure, ungodly peer alignments, or digital indoctrination, the "virtue" (the raw spiritual power and purity) of the child is siphoned out. This is the "Seed Bank" being emptied to fuel the enemy's systems.

**The Decay Inflow:** Conversely, the "systemic decay" of the world, anxiety, perversion, confusion, and foundational corruption, is pumped back into the child. The child becomes a "host" for frequencies that do not belong to their original Kingdom design.

**Digital Gateways and the Cultural Fog:** The "cultural fog" uses digital platforms to bypass the natural "Atmospheric Shield" of the home. When a child engages with content or connections that carry "sexual altars" or "anti Kingdom frequencies," a digital handshake occurs. In the spirit, this is viewed as an **Unauthorized Covenant**. These gateways allow the thief to enter the "Kingdom Estate" of the family without ever breaking a physical door.

Bible says, **1 Corinthians 6:16-17** "Do you not know that he who is joined to a harlot is one body with her? For 'the two,' He says, 'shall become one flesh.' But he who is joined to the Lord is one spirit with Him."

This means to glue or cement together. This is the mechanical definition of a merger. Paul is explaining that a spiritual and physical "union" creates a single functional system. When a child's soul is "glued" to a dark frequency, whether through a person, a screen, or a "cultural trend" they become "one body" with that system. The "systemic decay" of the "harlot" (the world system) begins to flow into the child because they are now legally connected.

The Mother of Lions must use her legislative authority to "un glue" (dismantle) these mergers, insisting that the child be "joined" only to the Lord, thereby ensuring the pipeline only carries the "one spirit" of Kingdom life.

## Legislative Action: Dismantling the Merger

**The Writ of Severance:** You must formally "sue" for the dissolution of these illegal mergers in the Court of Heaven.

**The Frequency Jam:** Use your altar to create a "mismatch" between your child's spirit and the world's signal, making the connection impossible to maintain.

**The Declaration:** "I strike the Gavel and I decree an immediate SEVERANCE of every illegal spiritual merger in my children's lives! I dismantle every unauthorized covenant formed through digital gateways or cultural fog! I break the glue of ungodly soul ties! I command the siphoning pipeline to be CUT and the virtue of my bloodline to be RESTORED! My children are not one with the decay of this world; they are joined to the Lord and one spirit with Him! Every 'harlot' system is evicted from their destiny! In Jesus' Name!"

**The Mother's Counter Strike:** As a Mother of Lions, you identify these siphons not as "growing pains," but as illegal incursions. Your role is to enforce the **Shadow of the Almighty**, a spiritual blackout that makes your children's Seed Bank invisible to the siphoning agents of the enemy.

## The Mother's Counter Strike: The Strategic Blackout

In the traditional mindset, parental protection is often viewed as a defensive or reactive posture comforting a child after a blow has been dealt. However, the **Mother of Lions** operates through a "Counter Strike" mentality. She refuses to categorize behavioral shifts, spiritual lethargy, or the "theft of innocence" as mere "growing pains" or inevitable phases of adolescence. Instead, she identifies them as **Illegal Incursions**, unauthorized border crossings into a sovereign Kingdom Estate.

**The Enforcement of the Spiritual Blackout**, When an incursion is detected, the Mother of Lions does not just "pray for help"; she enforces a **Spiritual Blackout**. In military terms, a blackout is used to deny the enemy the ability to see their target, rendering their precision guided weapons useless. By invoking the **Shadow of the Almighty**, you are creating a "cloaking field" over your children's Seed Bank.

**Radar Jamming:** The siphoning agents of the enemy rely on "tracking frequencies" the ability to locate a child's vulnerabilities through their digital footprint or generational echoes. Your counter strike "jams" these signals. You are declaring that your children's destinies are now **encrypted** within the secret place.

**Denying the "Target Lock":** By moving your children under the "Shadow," you make them invisible to the "Star Gazers" and "Herods" of this age. If the enemy cannot see the light, he cannot build a siphon to drain it.

**Offensive Shielding: The Gavel of the Altar,** A counter strike is offensive in nature. You are not waiting for the enemy to strike; you are preemptively striking the "legal grounds" the enemy uses to gain access.

**Judicial Eviction:** You use the "Gavel of your Altar" to issue an immediate eviction notice to any monitoring spirit or "familiar frequency" that has been hovering over your lineage. You aren't asking them to leave; you are legislating their removal based on the **Standard of Holiness** you have established in your home.

**The Frequency of the Lion:** As you roar in the spirit, you release a vibration that is discordant with the "systemic decay" of the world. This frequency creates a "No Go Zone" for siphoning agents. They find the atmosphere of your household too "hot" and too "weighted with Kavod" to remain.

The Bible says, **Isaiah 49:25** "But thus saith the Lord, Even the captives of the mighty shall be taken away, and the prey of the terrible shall be delivered: for **I will contend with him that contendeth with thee, and I will save thy children.**"

This is the **Statute of Divine Contention**. It reveals that when a Mother of Lions takes her place, she is not fighting alone. The word "contend" is a legal term meaning to "conduct a lawsuit." When you launch your counter strike, you are initiating a Heavenly Lawsuit against the siphoning agents. You are telling the Court of Heaven: *"These children are Kingdom assets; the enemy's incursion is a breach of contract."* God then becomes the Lead Litigator, ensuring that even if the children were "prey," they are legally delivered because the Mother enforced the "Blackout" of the Shadow.

## Legislative Action: The Counter Strike Protocol

**Execute the Blackout:** Formally decree that your children's identities, potentials, and "Seed Banks" are now **Invisible** to every demonic monitoring system.

**The Frequency Lock:** Command the "Sound of the Lion" to vibrate through your home, shattering the "digital telescopes" of the enemy.

**The Declaration:** "I strike the Gavel and I launch a Mother's Counter Strike! I refuse to call the enemy's theft a 'phase'! I identify every siphoning agent as an illegal incursion! I enforce the Shadow of the Almighty as a total Spiritual Blackout over my children! I decree that their Seed Bank is now encrypted and invisible to the Star Gazers! I jam every demonic radar and I break every target lock! The Lord contends with those who contend with my lineage! My children are delivered, hidden, and SECURE! In Jesus' Name!"

## The Psalm 91 Canopy: The Sterile Environment

To protect the Seed Bank, you must provide a "Canopy of Preservation." In the natural world, a seed bank must be kept in a climate controlled, sterile environment to ensure its future viability. Spiritually, the Altar of the Mother provides this climate.

**Neutralizing the Arrow:** Psalm 91 speaks of the "terror by night" and the "arrow that flies by day." These represent the targeted spiritual attacks aimed at a child's identity and purity. By standing at your altar, you create a canopy that these arrows cannot penetrate. You are legislating a "Bio demonically Secure" zone where your children can grow without being "stained by the night."

**Preserving the Morning Phase:** Most siphoning attempts happen during the "Morning Phase", the formative years of 0 to 20. By enforcing the Canopy, you ensure their star does not **flicker** or burn out early. You are holding their light in trust, declaring that it will not be traded for the "temporary relevance" of a compromised culture, but will be preserved until it achieves **Noon Day strength**.

**Psalm 91:1, 4** "He that dwelleth in the secret place of the most High shall abide under the shadow of the Almighty... He shall cover thee with his feathers, and under his wings shalt thou trust: his truth shall be thy shield and buckler."

The "Shadow of the Almighty" is the ultimate **anti siphoning protocol**. In a shadow, there is no direct line of sight. When you move your children under this canopy, you are "encrypting" their Seed Bank. The "feathers and wings" mentioned are not merely poetic; they represent the **Judicial Covering** of a Mother of Lions who has used her authority to hide her lineage. Under this canopy, the "truth" becomes a "shield and buckler", a mechanical defense that deflects the "illegal mergers" of the age.

## Legislative Action: The Audit of the Bank

**Plug the Leaks:** Identify any "premature exposure" in your household (media, associations, or environments) and issue a **Writ of Non Interference**.

**Seal the Vault:** Use the "Order of Sprinkling of the Blood of Jesus" to seal the eyes, ears, and gates of your children's lives.

**The Declaration:** "I strike the Gavel and I declare the Seed Bank of my children is SECURE! I reject the siphon of premature exposure! I dismantle every illegal spiritual merger attempted against their youth! I enforce the Psalm 91 Canopy over their spirits; they are hidden in the Secret Place where no scavenger can find them! Their light shall not be traded! Their virtue shall not be drained! I preserve them for their Noon Day Authority, and I decree that their star shall rise with absolute, shadowless strength! In Jesus' Name!"

## C. The Anatomy of the Protector: Healing the Source

The effectiveness of a protector is entirely dependent on the integrity of their own foundation. In the spirit realm, authority is not merely taken; it is authorized by alignment. If a mother attempts to guard her children's "Seed Bank" while her own "Safe" is still breached, she is attempting to enforce a law she is currently breaking. Recognizing that the "siphoning" of a child's light often happens through the echoes of the mother's own unhealed past is the first step toward becoming a truly impenetrable shield.

**Closing the Portals: The Internal Defense,** Protecting the next generation requires the mother to first **repossess her own destiny**. If a mother has not dismantled the "sexual altars," "illegal mergers," or "foundational corruption" in her own history, she inadvertently leaves a "back door" open. In the spirit, these unhealed areas act as open portals, points of entry where the thief can bypass the child's defenses by using the mother's unresolved frequencies as a key.

**The Celestial Shield:** When the Mother of Lions undergoes the "Sanitization Protocol" herself, she becomes a **Celestial Shield**. Her healing is not just for her own comfort; it is a strategic closing of the gates. She understands that her internal stability, her "Noon Day" authority, is the primary defense for her children's future.

**Ending the Echoes:** By addressing "The Anatomy of Regret" and the "Mother's Warning" from her own lineage, she stops the resonance. The enemy can no longer use the mother's past to "ping" the child's future. When the source is healed, the protection is absolute.

## The Legacy of Light: Training the Bloodline to Stay Lit,

You are not just protecting your children; you are **Training the Bloodline**. You are teaching them that their "shine" is not a lucky accident, but a protected inheritance. This is the establishment of a **Kingdom Estate** that operates under its own legislative rules.

**Covenantal Consistency:** Your children learn that their protection is a covenant signed by your consistency and sealed by your spiritual governance. They see that the "Standard of Holiness" is not a burden, but the very thing that keeps their star from flickering.

**The "No Fall" Estate:** You are creating a lineage where the "fall" is no longer a generational expectation. In this estate, no star falls on your watch because the "Atmospheric Shield" is maintained with precision. You are teaching them never to trade their light for the "shadows" of temporary cultural relevance.

Bible says, **Psalm 51:10, 13** "Create in me a clean heart, O God; and renew a right spirit within me... Then will I teach transgressors thy ways; and sinners shall be converted unto thee."

This is the **Protector's Protocol**. David understood that he could not "teach" or "govern" effectively until his own heart was "Sanitized." The "Clean Heart" is the closed portal. Once the Mother of Lions is renewed and her spirit is "Right" (legally aligned), she gains the legislative right to "teach" and "convert" her environment. Her personal healing becomes the blueprint for the entire bloodline's survival.

**The Decree of the Healed Source:** "I strike the Gavel and I declare that every portal in my past is CLOSED! I dismantle every sexual altar and every foundational corruption that seeks to echo into my children's future! I repossess my destiny and I establish my own Noon Day Authority! I am a healed source, and my stability is the shield of my bloodline. I sign the covenant of their protection with my consistency. In my estate, no star shall fall, and no light shall be traded for darkness! My lineage stays lit! In Jesus' Name!"

### The "Star Preservation" Decree

"I strike the Gavel and I authorize the 'Sanitization of the Atmosphere' over my star and the stars of my seed! I invoke Daniel 12:3 and I decree that we shall NOT be dimmed, we shall NOT be dampened, and we shall NOT be displaced!

"I issue a 'Restraining Order' against every Herod entity and every Star Hunter tracking our light! I 'Veto' the Marine Fog and the Smog of Compromise! I decree that our Luminosity Quotient is rising to the level of 'Noon Day' Excellence!

"We are Navigational Assets to the Kingdom! We do not argue with darkness; we occupy it! I decree that our stars are 'Legally Protected' by the Blood of the Lamb and 'Strategically Positioned' by the Lion of Judah! Our light is Permanent, our path is Clear, and the King is Glorified! In Jesus' Name!"

## Warfare prayer, chapter 5: the mother as a guardian of destiny

### Judicial Activation Decrees for the Next Generation

This Warfare is designed for the **Guardian of the Bloodline**. As a mother and a leader, you are the **Womb-Gatekeeper**. These decrees are not pleas; they are **Judicial Injunctions** to secure the potential of your children against systemic siphoning.

**Category I: Guiding & "Catching" Potential (The Redirect)**

**1. The Divine Sonar Decree:**

"I activate my maternal sonar to 'catch' the early frequencies of my children's divine potential. I decree that no gift, talent, or prophetic inclination in them shall remain hidden or dormant. I receive the wisdom to redirect every 'wandering' energy into its correct professional and spiritual orbit." **( Proverbs 22:6)**

**2. The Alignment of the Bloodline:**

"I legislatively override every 'hereditary detour' attempting to pull my children toward the mistakes of the past. I decree that their steps are ordered by the Lord and synchronized with the **Coordinate of Truth.** They shall not start at my floor; they shall start at my ceiling." **( Psalm 37:23)**

**Category II: Shielding from Cultural Theft (The Shield)**

**3. The Veto of Cultural Contamination:**

"I issue a **Judicial Veto** against the 'Normalized Evils' of this generation. I forbid the spirit of the age, the 'Smog of Compromise,' and toxic social frequencies from siphoning the identity of my children. I decree they are immune to the 'Marine Fogs' of confusion that blur the lines between right and wrong." **( Romans 12:2)**

**4. The No-Fly Zone Over the Mind:**

"I establish a 'No-Fly Zone' over the imaginations and digital gateways of my children. I command every 'Star-Hunter' and monitoring spirit seeking to track their innocence to be struck with judicial blindness. My children's minds are Kingdom Estates, strictly off-limits to demonic surveillance." **( Isaiah 54:13)**

**Category III: Dismantling Legacy Siphons (The Recovery)**

**5. Breaking the "Star-Hunter" Contract:**

"I cancel every 'illegal merger' formed against my children's future by ancestral setbacks or mother's warnings that went unheeded in previous generations. I decree that the siphoning of my bloodline's virtue stops with me. I legislatively close every door that allowed 'Star-Thieves' to enter my family tree." **(Galatians 3:13)**

**6. Repossessing the Seed-Bank:**

"I move into the 'Marine Vaults' and the 'Deep' to repossess every hijacked dream and potential stolen from my bloodline. I decree the immediate release of my children's professional authority, academic excellence, and spiritual rank. What was stolen from the fathers is now being restored through the Mother-Guardian." **(Scripture: Joel 2:25)**

**Category IV: The Bold Protector (The Standard)**

**7. Establishing the High-Noon Standard:**

"I set a **Standard of Excellence** in my home that the night cannot comprehend. I decree that my children shall carry a frequency of integrity so high that the 'Herod spirits' in their schools and future workplaces will have no legal ground to touch them. I am building a fortress of character that secures their legacy." **(Scripture: Isaiah 59:19)**

**8. The Decree of the Fixed Star Offspring:**

"I declare that my children are not 'flickering' lights; they are **Fixed Stars** commissioned to rule their generation. I forbid them from becoming 'wandering stars' of inconsistency. I decree stability, reliability, and absolute focus over their destinies." **(Scripture: Daniel 12:3)**

**Category V: Final Maternal Governance (The Gavel)**

**9. The Covenant of Peace:**

"I legislate a 'Covenant of Peace' over my household. I forbid family chaos, divorce, or foundational cracks from manifesting in the next generation. I decree that the 'GPS of the Spirit' is now the primary navigational tool for every member of my house." **(Scripture: Isaiah 54:10)**

**10. The Gavel Falls on the Bloodline:**

"The Gavel has fallen. The training of my bloodline is now a settled judicial decree. I arise as a **Bold Protector**, I shine as a **Guardian of Destiny**, and I secure the future of my children with the weight of the King's *Kavod*. My seed is blessed, my legacy is untouchable, and the standard is set. It is finished!" **(Scripture: Psalm 112:2)**

# Chapter 6: Celestial Mapping & Strategy

## Navigating the Complexities of Global Influence

### A. Spiritual Cartography: Reading the Atmosphere

Learning to "read" the atmosphere of a city or organization before you enter it.

**Spiritual Cartography** is the high level discipline of discerning the invisible "climate" and "legal structures" of a territory before you set foot in it or invest your resources there. Just as a natural map shows mountains and valleys, a spiritual map reveals the **strongholds** (the obstacles) and the **open gates** (the opportunities) within a city, a boardroom, or an organization.

To "read" an atmosphere is to recognize that no environment is neutral. Every city or corporation has a "frequency", a prevailing spirit that dictates how people think, how money moves, and whether a "Star" will be welcomed or pursued by a "Herod."

### The Deep Insight: Discerning the "Prince" of the Territory

In the realm of governance, you must realize that you are not just dealing with people; you are dealing with the **principality** behind the people. If you enter a city to do business without first mapping its spiritual layout, you may find yourself fighting "shadows", delays, unexplainable technical failures, or sudden character assassinations, that are actually systemic spiritual defenses.

**The Atmospheric Pressure:** Some organizations feel "heavy" because they are governed by the **Smog of Compromise**.

**The Marine Influence:** Some coastal cities or liquid markets are governed by "Marine Fogs" of confusion that make even the clearest contracts turn murky.

**The Scriptural Foundation,** The primary biblical precedent for Spiritual Cartography is found in the book of **Daniel**:

"Then he said, 'Do you know why I have come to you? And now I must return to fight with the **prince of Persia**; and when I have gone forth, indeed the **prince of Greece** will come.' **Daniel 10:20**

**The Verse Breakdown:**

**Geographic Assignment:** Notice that these spiritual entities are named after territories (**Persia** and **Greece**). This confirms that spirits have "jurisdiction."

**The Delayed Breakthrough:** Daniel's answer was delayed for 21 days not because his prayer was weak, but because he was dealing with an **Atmospheric Gatekeeper**.

**The Legislative Counter Move:** Daniel had to engage in a specific spiritual frequency (fasting and mourning) to "map" the resistance and authorize the angelic intervention (Michael) to clear the path.

**Strategic Application for the Leader:** Before you sign a contract, launch a conference, or move your family to a new location, you must execute a **Cartographic Audit**:

**Observation:** What is the "normalized evil" in this place? Is it pride, greed, or a spirit of "stagnation"? Is it homosexuality, additions, Premature death, Violence, Poverty etc.

**Frequency Check:** Does your spirit feel "muffled" when you speak, or does your light expand?

## The Frequency Check: Expansion vs. Muffling

In the realm of **Spiritual Cartography**, your spirit acts as a highly sensitive sonar system. Because you are a "Star" (a luminary body), you naturally emit a specific frequency of truth, integrity, and authority. When you enter a new environment, be it a physical city, a digital platform, or a corporate boardroom that environment will either **resonate** with your frequency or attempt to **dampen** it.

**The "Muffled" Spirit: Identifying Atmospheric Interference,** A "muffled" spirit feels like speaking underwater or trying to shine a light through thick, heavy velvet. You may notice:

**Mental Fog:** Sudden confusion or "word loss" during high stakes conversations.

**Drainage:** Feeling exhausted after a simple meeting, as if the atmosphere literally "siphoned" your virtue.

**The "Muzzle" Effect:** A hesitation to speak the full truth, or a feeling that your ideas are falling on "deaf air" regardless of how well you present them.

This muffling is often the result of **The Smog of Compromise** or **Marine Fogs**. These are atmospheric defensive systems designed to protect the "status quo" of that territory from the disruptive light of a leader.

**The "Expanding" Light: The Sign of Territorial Submission,** When your light expands, you feel a "witness" in your spirit. The atmosphere feels thin, clear, and cooperative. You will experience:

**Flow:** Ideas come effortlessly, and your speech carries a "weight" (*Kavod*) that demands attention.

**Dominion:** You feel "larger" than the room. Instead of the environment changing you, you realize you are changing the environment.

**Acceleration:** Projects that take months elsewhere happen in days because the "Gates" of that territory have been legislatively opened to you.

**The Scriptural Foundation: The Resonating Atmosphere,** The most profound example of a "Frequency Check" occurs when two luminaries meet in a territory that recognizes the King:

The bible says, "And it happened, when Elizabeth heard the greeting of Mary, that the babe leaped in her womb; and Elizabeth was filled with the Holy Spirit." **Luke 1:41**

**The Verse Breakdown:**

**The Greeting (The Frequency):** Mary didn't need to explain her mandate; her voice carried the frequency of the "Bright and Morning Star."

**The Leap (The Expansion):** The atmosphere (and the "next generation" in the womb) immediately responded. There was no muffling; there was a **Frequency Match**.

**The Result:** The environment became "Sanitized" for the prophetic purpose to be spoken aloud.

**The Governor's Protocol: How to Shift the Frequency,** If you perform a check and find your spirit is being **muffled**, do not retreat. Instead, execute an **Atmospheric Override**:

**Stop Seeking Approval:** Muffling often happens when you try to "blend in." A star that tries to be a shadow loses its power.

**Raise the Volume of Your Integrity:** Integrity is a high frequency vibration. When you refuse to participate in the "Smog of Compromise," the atmosphere is forced to adjust to *you*.

**Decree the "No-Fly Zone":** Explicitly forbid any "monitoring spirit" or "Herod entity" from siphoning your energy.

**The Coordinate of Truth:** You are not in that room to fit into the atmosphere; you are there to be the **Climate Changer**. If the room feels dark, it is simply a legal signal that your "High Noon" authority is required.

**Judicial Positioning:** Once you identify the "Prince" (the dominant negative influence), you don't just "fight." You **legislatively override** it by decreeing a higher law, the Law of the Spirit of Life, over that specific coordinate.

**Judicial Positioning: The Legislative Override** In the manual of **Star Deliverance**, you must graduate from the mindset of a "spiritual foot soldier" to that of a **Celestial Governor**. A soldier fights for ground; a Governor *occupies* it by the power of the Law.

**Judicial Positioning** is the act of standing at a specific coordinate, whether it is your workplace, your home, or a city gate, and enforcing a higher legal reality that makes the "Prince" of that territory powerless to act against you.

**Identifying the "Prince" vs. The Human Face,** You must look past the difficult boss, the stagnant economy, or the rebellious child to see the **Principality** (the Prince) providing the "legal" energy for that behavior.

- If a boardroom is filled with lies, the "Prince" is the **Spirit of Deception**.
- If a family is stuck in poverty, the "Prince" is the **Spirit of Lack** or a **Marine Siphon**.

**The Protocol: From "Fighting" to "Legislating"** "Fighting" is reactive and exhausting. "Legislating" is proactive and authoritative. When you identify the dominant negative influence, you do not beg it to leave; you **Veto** its right to exist in your jurisdiction.

**The Lower Law:** The "Prince" operates on the laws of sin, death, and generational cycles.

**The Higher Law:** You operate on the **Law of the Spirit of Life**.

**The Scriptural Foundation: The Law of the Spirit of Life,** The primary legal precedent for this override is found in the "Constitution of Grace":

"For the **law of the Spirit of life** in Christ Jesus has made me free from the **law of sin and death**." **Romans 8:2**

**The Verse Breakdown:**

**Conflict of Laws:** This is a courtroom scene. Two laws are mentioned. In any judicial system, a **federal or supreme law** always overrides a local or lower law.

**The Superior Jurisdiction:** The "Law of the Spirit of Life" is the supreme law of the Kingdom. When this law is cited and enforced, the lower "Law of Sin and Death" (the Prince's jurisdiction) is rendered **unconstitutional** and unenforceable.

**The Absolute Verdict:** It does not say the lower law "asked" to leave; it says the higher law "made me free." It is a forced eviction based on legal superiority.

**How to Execute a Legislative Decree,** When you stand at your "Coordinate of Truth," you must speak with **Judicial Precision**.

**The Identification:** "I identify the 'Prince of Confusion' attempting to muffle the strategy in this organization."

**The Citation:** "I cite the Law of the Spirit of Life (Romans 8:2) as the governing authority over this coordinate."

**The Override:** "By my authority as a Celestial Governor, I **Veto** the decree of stagnation. I declare a **No-Fly Zone** against monitoring spirits. I legislate clarity, acceleration, and Kingdom excellence into this atmosphere."

**The Governor's Secret: The Gavel of Consistency,** A judicial decree only works if the judge is in **"Prophetic Rank."** If you are practicing the same compromise you are trying to override, your "Gavel" will have no sound. But when your life is "Sanitized," your decree becomes a **Legislative Instrument** that the Prince of that territory must obey.

**Verdict:** You don't have to win the "fight" if you have already won the **legal argument**. Stop swinging a sword at shadows and start dropping the Gavel of the Word.

**The Governor's Secret:** A star does not ask for permission to shine; it simply occupies the space it has mapped out. When you understand the map, you can walk through "enemy territory" and remain completely untouched by its climate.

**B. The Midnight Watch:**

How to use the "Night Seasons" for strategic planning rather than falling victim to the dark.

**The Midnight Watch: Strategic Planning in the Night Season**, In the architecture of **Star Deliverance**, the "Night" is not merely a period of time; it is a **strategic window**. Most people view the night or a "Night Season" of life as a time of vulnerability, fear, or forced inactivity. However, for the **Celestial Governor**, the night is when the "Star" is most visible and when the most profound legislation is written.

The **Midnight Watch** is the practice of positioning yourself while the world (and your competition) sleeps, to capture the "coordinates" for your next move.

**The Night as a "Womb" for Strategy,** The night is the realm of the **unseen and the potential**. In the natural world, seeds germinate in the dark; in the spiritual world, high level strategies are birthed in the silence of the night watch.

While the "Night Season" of history brings "Marine Fogs" and confusion, the Governor uses this lack of external noise to hear the "Frequency of the Spirit" with absolute clarity.

Instead of falling victim to the "Star Hunters" who track destinies in the dark, you use the night to **re route your path**, making your next moves invisible to those who wish to sabotage you.

**Moving from Victim to Watchman,** The "Victim of the Night" is terrified of the shadows. The "Watchman of the Night" understands that **darkness is simply the absence of a decree.** Strategic planning during the Midnight Watch allows you to:

**Anticipate the Dawn:** You don't wait for the sun to rise to decide what to do; you have already legislated the day's victory before the first light hits the horizon.

**Identify the "Herod Spirits":** In the quiet, the subtle movements of your enemies become loud. You can detect the "vibration" of compromise or betrayal before it manifests in the boardroom.

**The Scriptural Foundation: The Midnight Decree,** The primary biblical precedent for strategic night time legislation is found in the life of **King David**:

"At midnight I will rise to give thanks to You, because of Your **righteous judgments**." **Psalm 119:62**

**The Verse Breakdown:**

**The Intentional Rise:** David didn't just "stay awake" due to anxiety; he **authorized himself** to rise. He took control of his sleep cycle for a higher purpose.

**Focus on Judgments:** He wasn't just praying general prayers; he was focusing on **Judgments** (Legal Verdicts). He was aligning his mind with the "Supreme Court of Heaven" at the very hour when the "Night Season" was at its peak.

**The Result:** Because David mastered the Midnight Watch, he was always ten steps ahead of his enemies. He had the "Mapping" of the kingdom settled before his opponents even woke up.

**Practical Application: How to Use the Night Watch,** To use the Night Season for strategic planning, you must execute the **Watchman's Protocol**:

**The Audit of the Day:** Review the day's "Muffling" incidents. Where did you feel your light dim?

**The Legislative Session:** Do not just "think", write. Use the silence to draft your "Manual of Governance" for the upcoming season.

**The Pre-emptive Strike:** Use the night to decree a **"No-Fly Zone"** over your children's dreams and your business assets. While the "Star Hunters" are looking for your past, you are legislating your future.

**The Governor's Secret:** The reason the stars are placed in the night sky is not just for beauty, but for **navigation**. If there were no night, the traveler would have no constant point of reference. Your "Night Season" is not a sign of defeat; it is the only time your **Prophetic Rank** can be used to guide others through the fog.

**Stop trying to "survive" the night. Start using it to govern the morning.**

### C. Identifying Star-Trackers:

Recognizing external systems (both human and spiritual) designed to monitor and redirect your progress. In the celestial economy, a "Star" is not just a light; it is a **sign**. Your progress signals a shift in the atmosphere and a threat to the established "Night Season." Because of this, you must understand that your growth is not being watched merely by fans or critics, it is being **tracked** by sophisticated systems designed to calculate your trajectory and divert you from your "Prophetic Seat."

**Star Trackers** are external entities, both in the human marketplace and the spiritual realm, that monitor your "brightness" to determine when to strike, when to siphoning, and when to offer a "Smog of Compromise."

**The Two Levels of Tracking:**

**Human Systems (The Corporate & Social):** These are individuals or organizations that monitor your innovation, your influence, and your "Star-Power." They don't just want to compete; they want to **redirect your energy** into their systems, siphoning your ideas and leaving you with the "soot" of their overhead.

**Spiritual Systems (The "Herod Spirits"):** These are demonic monitoring systems that track the "birth" of new mantles and leadership levels. Just as Herod tracked the star to find the child, these spirits track your "Prophetic Rank" to see if they can abort your legacy before it reaches full strength.

This framework explains that as you rise in leadership and influence, you are being watched on two distinct levels. One wants your **output**, while the other wants your **end**.

## The Human Level: The Corporate Siphon

This level is managed by people and organizations. They recognize your "Star-Power", your unique talent, innovation, and influence, often before you do.

Instead of helping you grow, their goal is to **harvest** you. They want to plug your light into their machines to keep their systems running. In this exchange, they take the "gold" of your ideas and leave you with the "soot", the burnout, the heavy administrative work, and the stress of their problems. You end up doing the work, but they own the results.

## The Spiritual Level: The Herod Spirit

This is a deeper, more aggressive form of tracking. Just as King Herod tracked the star to find and destroy a future King while he was still a baby, these spiritual systems monitor your "Prophetic Rank."

They aren't looking for your money or your labor; they are looking for your **Destiny**. They track the "birth" of new levels of authority in your life and try to "abort" your mission while it is still new and vulnerable. Their goal is to make sure your legacy is destroyed before it ever reaches full strength.

## The Collision: When Systems Work Together

The most difficult seasons occur when these two levels work in harmony against you. This is the "overlap."

**The Physical Trap:** The human system creates a crisis, like a legal battle, a heavy workload, or a toxic environment. This keeps your hands tied and your mind distracted.

**The Spiritual Attack:** While you are distracted by the physical stress, the spiritual system attacks your spirit. It uses your exhaustion to make you want to quit, surrender your "Star," or walk away from your calling entirely.

In this state, the corporate system acts as the cage, while the spiritual system acts as the hunter. One drains your strength so the other can finish the job.

## The Way Out: Delivering the Star

To protect your legacy, you must recognize which system is speaking to you. You cannot solve a spiritual tracking problem with a better contract, and you cannot solve a legal "siphon" problem with prayer alone.

**Deliverance** happens when you:

**Guard the "Birth":** Keep your biggest ideas and "new mantles" hidden until they are strong enough to survive the light.

**Use Your Veto Power:** Recognize when a system is taking more than it gives and have the courage to disconnect your energy from it.

**Maintain Integrity:** When your professional and personal systems are clean, there is no "soot" for these trackers to use against you.

**Identifying the "Tracking Frequency",** You can recognize that you are being tracked when you notice:

**Unusual Patterns of Resistance:** Every time you prepare for a "Rank" increase (a promotion, a book launch, a new level of consecration), a specific, recurring obstacle appears.

**The "Copycat" Signal:** People or entities suddenly begin mimicking your "frequency" or siphoning your specific language to redirect your audience or resources to themselves.

**Atmospheric Surveillance:** A feeling of being "watched" or "heaviness" that occurs specifically when you are drafting new strategies during your **Midnight Watch**.

**The Scriptural Foundation: The Herod Tracking System,** The primary biblical precedent for Star Tracking is the reaction of the status quo to a new "Prophetic Governor":

"And he Herod sent them to Bethlehem and said, 'Go and search carefully for the young Child... that I may come and worship Him also.' ...And behold, the **star** which they had seen in the East went before them, till it came and stood over where the young Child was." **Matthew 2:8-9**

**The Verse Breakdown:**

**The False Intent:** Herod used "religious" language ("worship Him") to hide a **hit contract**. Star-trackers often wear the mask of mentors, partners, or "interested parties."

**The Systematic Search:** Herod didn't guess; he "searched carefully." He used the data of the star's appearance to calculate the timing of his attack.

**The Redirection:** Herod's goal was to redirect the journey of the wise men to serve his own agenda of destruction.

**The Governor's Counter-Strategy: Stealth and Re-Routing,** Once you identify that you are being tracked, you must execute the **"No-Fly Zone" Protocol**:

**Stealth Mode:** Stop broadcasting your "coordinates" (your plans, your inner circles, your deep strategies) on public frequencies. Be visible for your work, but **invisible** in your process.

**Legislative Sanitization:** Decree a "Judicial Blindness" over monitoring spirits. Use your authority to scramble the "tracking signals" of those who wish to siphoning your virtue.

**The Divine Detour:** Just as the wise men were warned in a dream to "return by another way," you must be willing to **re-route** your professional and spiritual maneuvers to stay ahead of the "Herod spirits."

**The Coordinate of Truth:** A star is only "trackable" if it remains in a predictable orbit. When you move by the "GPS of the Spirit," you become a **Moving Target** that the systems of the night cannot lock onto.

**They can see your light, but they must never be allowed to calculate your source.**

## Warfare prayer, chapter six: celestial mapping & strategy

## Target: Atmospheric Cleansing & Strategic Stealth

### Category I: Spiritual Cartography (The Mapping)

### 1. The Decree of Sight:

"In the name of the Lord, I command my spiritual eyes to be 'Sanitized' from the soot of the world. I receive the high level frequency to map out the 'Princes' and 'Atmospheric Gatekeepers' of this city/organization before I invest my seed. No hidden snare shall remain unmapped in my path." **(Ephesians 1:18)**

### 2. The Dismantling of the Prince:

"I identify the dominant negative influence (stagnation/deception/greed) over this coordinate. I cite the **Law of the Spirit of Life** and I Veto its legal right to operate against my mission. I declare this coordinate a Kingdom Outpost, and I legislatively override the local atmosphere of compromise." **(Romans 8:2)**

**Category II: The Midnight Watch (The Timing)**

**3. The Command of the Morning:**

"I take my seat in the Midnight Watch. I decree that my sleep shall not be a time of siphoning, but a 'Womb of Strategy.' I command the morning to take hold of the ends of the earth and shake the wicked out of it. My dawn shall not find me unprepared; it shall find me positioned." **(Job 38:12-13)**

**4. The Frequency Alignment:**

"I check my spiritual frequency now. I reject every 'Muffling' spirit that attempts to dampen my authority in the boardroom or the sanctuary. I declare my light is **Expanding.** I am not a resident of the atmosphere; I am the Climate Changer. Every ear in this environment is now legally opened to the weight of my *Kavod*." **( Luke 1:41)**

**Category III: Neutralizing Star-Trackers (The Stealth)**

**5. The Blindness Decree:**

"I invoke 'Judicial Blindness' upon every 'Herod spirit' and 'Star-Hunter' tracking my trajectory. I scramble their spiritual sonar and digital monitoring systems. I decree that my deep strategies are hidden in the secret place of the Most High, visible for impact, but **invisible for sabotage." ( Psalm 91:1)**

**6. Breaking the "Herod" Contract:**

"I cancel every false 'worship' contract, every human or system that has approached me with a mask of partnership but a heart of siphoning. I decree that their search for my source shall end in confusion. I am re-routing my path by the GPS of the Spirit, and they shall not find the coordinate of my potential." **( Matthew 2:12)**

**Category IV: Territorial Dominion (The Governance)**

**7. The No-Fly Zone:**

"I establish a 'No-Fly Zone' over my family, my business, and my prophetic seat. I forbid the 'Marine Fogs' of confusion from hovering over my decision, making process. I am a Fixed Star, and I declare that my orbit is protected from every wandering spirit of distraction." **( Isaiah 54:17)**

**8. The Repossession of Siphoned Virtue:**

"I issue a celestial summons for the immediate return of every idea, client, and resource that was siphoned by 'Star-Trackers' in my previous seasons of ignorance. I demand a seven-fold judicial restoration of my marketplace virtue, now!" **( Proverbs 6:31)**

**Category V: Final Activation (The Gavel)**

**9. The Decree of the Fixed Star:**

"I refuse to be a 'Flickering' leader. I move from a seasonal influence to a **Constitutional Appointment.** I decree that my rank is established in the heavens, and no earthly 'Prince' has the jurisdiction to veto my promotion." **(Daniel 12:3)**

**10. The Gavel Falls:**

"The Gavel has fallen. The night season of being tracked and siphoned is over. I arise in my **Prophetic Rank**, I shine with the frequency of the King, and I govern my territory with absolute integrity and power. It is finished!" **( Isaiah 60:1)**

# Chapter 7: The Judicial Protocols of Recovery

This chapter shifts from defense to **Judicial Aggression**. In the Kingdom, recovery is not an emotional plea; it is a legal repossession. When a "Star" has been tracked and siphoned, there is a trail of "Cargo" (virtue, time, and resources) that has been illegally moved into foreign vaults. Chapter 7 provides the protocol to get it back.

## A. The Divine Audit: Assessing the Leakage

The **Divine Audit** is the moment you stop guessing why you are tired and start looking at the "spiritual receipts" of your life. It is an intensive investigation to find the gap between what God officially authorized for you (your **Constitutional Appointment**) and what you are actually experiencing (**Current Reality**).

If you are supposed to be a "Fixed Star", steady, bright, and immovable, but you find yourself "flickering," it means there is a **leak**. This isn't just "bad luck"; it is a mechanical failure in your life's systems.

## The Three Forms of Leakage

Leakage is the silent, unauthorized transfer of your "virtue" into systems that didn't earn it.

**Health Leakage (The Trade):** This is when your physical vitality is traded for stress. It often happens through **"Suicidal Attachments"**, connections to people, jobs, or habits that are literally killing you to keep themselves alive. You aren't just "tired"; you are being siphoned.

**Financial Leakage (The Dissolve):** This is money that disappears despite your hard work. It's the "Marine Siphon" effect, where wealth seems to evaporate or "dissolve" before it can be used for your legacy. It's not a spending problem; it's a spiritual drainage problem.

**Joy Leakage (The Muffle):** This is the most dangerous because it attacks your "engine." When your joy is siphoned, you become **"muffled."** You are still moving, but the sound of your life has lost its power. You are exhausted because you are running on empty.

## The Deep Insight: The "Missing Goods" Ledger

In a legal audit, you look for what *should* be in the warehouse versus what is *actually* on the shelves. Spiritually, the Audit reveals your **Missing Goods**.

If the "Ledger" says you were appointed to be a leader of nations, but you are currently struggling to lead your own day, the Audit identifies the **Foundational Crack**. It finds the "Illegal Merger", the place where you accidentally joined your life to a system that has a legal right to drain you. You cannot repossess your peace until you identify exactly where it left the building.

## The Scriptural Law of Joel 2:25

The verse in Joel is not just a poetic comfort; it is a **Judicial Verdict**. It is the Supreme Court of Heaven acknowledging that a crime was committed and ordering a settlement.

### The Categorization of the Theft

Notice that there isn't just one type of locust; there are four. This shows that the "Tracking Systems" use different methods to drain you:

**The Chewing Locust:** This is the slow drain. It eats at your health and joy bit by bit so you don't notice it until you are hollow.

**The Consuming Locust:** This is the sudden hit. It's the financial "crash" or the "scandal" that tries to swallow your reputation in one bite.

**The Swarming/Crawling Locusts:** These are the social and corporate systems that overwhelm you with "overhead" and "soot" until you are buried under the weight of other people's demands.

To explain these four "locusts" is to understand that your life is under a sophisticated, multi-layered siege. These aren't just bugs; they are **specialized retrieval systems** sent to collect the "virtue" and "energy" of your Star. Each one targets a different speed and a different area of your life to ensure that if one doesn't stop you, the next one will.

## The Chewing Locust: The Master of the Slow Drain

The "Chewer" is the most dangerous because it is **silent**. It doesn't create a crisis; it creates a "habit" of exhaustion.

**The Method:** It operates through the small, daily compromises. It's the extra hour of work you weren't supposed to give, the toxic conversation you let linger, or the "minor" stress you've accepted as normal.

**The Target:** Your **Health and Joy**. It chews at the edges of your vitality. You don't wake up one day "hollow", you wake up one day and realize you haven't felt a spark of genuine joy in three years.

**The Deep Result:** It turns a "Fixed Star" into a "Flickering Star" by slowly thinning out the fuel. By the time you notice the damage, the Chewer has already moved on to your core.

## The Consuming Locust: The Specialist of the Sudden Hit

Unlike the Chewer, the "Consumer" wants everything **now**. It is designed to create a "Total System Failure."

**The Method:** This is the "Marine Siphon" in action. It's the sudden financial emergency that wipes out your savings, the legal "ambush," or the "scandal" (often fabricated or exaggerated) aimed at your reputation.

**The Target:** Your **Platform and Provision**. It targets the things you've built over decades, attempting to swallow them in a single weekend.

**The Deep Result:** It aims to shock your system into a state of "Abortion." It wants the pressure to be so high that you "rescind" your mantle just to make the pain stop. It's a high-velocity attack on your Star-Power.

## The Crawling Locust: The Architect of Bureaucracy

The "Crawler" doesn't eat you; it **covers** you. It works by slowing your momentum until you simply stop moving.

**The Method:** It operates through "Overhead" and "Soot." These are the endless, low-level tasks, the "red tape," and the "social obligations" that have nothing to do with your destiny. It's the "Illegal Merger" where you find yourself managing everyone else's problems while your own manuscript sits untouched.

**The Target:** Your **Time and Focus**. It makes the "Star" so heavy with Earthly "soot" that it can no longer stay in orbit.

**The Deep Result:** You become a "Prophetic Bureaucrat", someone who has the title and the rank but spends all their energy maintaining a system that actually siphons them.

## The Swarming Locust: The Force of Social Pressure

The "Swarmer" uses the power of the "Group" to overwhelm your individual light.

**The Method:** This is the "Corporate and Social" tracking system in full force. It's the "swarming" of opinions, the demands of the "crowd," and the pressure to conform to a system's "Cultural Carrier" expectations that don't align with your integrity.

**The Target:** Your **Identity and Distinction**. The swarm wants to blend you into the background. They don't want you to be a "Fixed Star"; they want you to be part of their "Cloud."

**The Deep Result:** It creates "Identity Leakage." You lose the "unique signal" of your prophetic rank because you are too busy trying to manage the noise of the swarm.

**The Deep Realization,** The "Divine Audit" reveals that these four locusts work in a sequence:

1. The **Swarmer** distracts you with people.
2. The **Crawler** weighs you down with tasks.
3. The **Chewer** drains your daily strength.
4. The **Consumer** waits for you to be weak enough to strike the final blow.

**The Judicial Verdict of Joel 2:25** is so powerful because it doesn't just "shoo" the bugs away, it acknowledges that you have been the victim of an organized, four-stage theft. When the Verdict is released, it stops the "Chewing," clears the "Soot," restores the "Swallowed Wealth," and silences the "Swarm" all at once.

### The Judicial Decree of Restoration

When the verse says, *"I will restore to you the years,"* it is a legal reversal. It acknowledges that **Time**, the one thing we think is gone forever, can be restored. In a normal court, if someone steals your car, they give you a car back. In the Divine Audit, if the "Herod Spirit" or the "Corporate Siphon" stole 10 years of your influence, the Decree doesn't just give you "new years"; it packs the **power and results** of those 10 years into your *now*. It is a total recovery of the "Missing Goods" with interest.

## The Verdict

The Audit proves that you haven't "lost" your star-power; it has simply been **misdirected**. Once the Audit is complete and the leaks are plugged, the "Siphon" loses its legal right to your energy, and the "Herod Spirit" is forced to pay back what it tried to abort.

## B. Filing a Celestial Petition: Precise Language for "Cargo" Recovery

Once the audit is complete, you do not "beg" for restoration; you **File a Petition**. In the Marine Kingdom, which governs "liquid assets" and hidden "vaults" at the bottom of the sea, you must use **Judicial Precision**.

**The Concept of "Cargo":** In spiritual cartography, your destiny is often viewed as a merchant ship carrying "Prophetic Cargo." If that ship was "wrecked" by a Marine Fog, your cargo is sitting in an illegal vault.

**The Precise Language:** You must cite the **Standard of Holiness** and the **Blood Covenant** as your legal standing to demand a "Writ of Mandamus", a court order to a lower official (a demonic gatekeeper) to perform their duty by releasing your goods.

Once the **Divine Audit** has identified the leakage and the specific locusts involved, you move from the "Assessment" phase to the **"Enforcement"** phase. In the spiritual realm, and specifically when dealing with the "Marine Kingdom" (which oversees the "flow" of wealth, influence, and liquid assets), you do not ask for a favor. You **File a Petition.**

This is a formal, legal process where you use the "Judicial Protocols" of heaven to demand the release of what is rightfully yours.

## The Concept of "Cargo": Your Sunken Destiny

In the spiritual legal system, your life's purpose is handled like a **Merchant Vessel**. This ship is loaded with "Prophetic Cargo", the health, finances, relationships, and "Star-Power" needed to fulfill your assignment.

**The Marine Fog:** This is a spiritual "Tracking System" that creates confusion and "muffles" your sight. Its goal is to cause a "Shipwreck", a moment in your life or career where everything seemed to go down.

**The Illegal Vault:** When a shipwreck occurs, the "Cargo" doesn't just disappear; it is "arrested" and stored in illegal underwater vaults. This is why you feel the weight of your potential, but you cannot "touch" it in your current reality. It is sitting at the bottom of a system that has no legal right to keep it.

## The Language of the "Writ of Mandamus"

To recover this cargo, you must use **Precise Judicial Language.** You are not appealing to the "mercy" of the thief; you are appealing to the **Authority of the Judge.**

**Your Legal Standing:** You don't file the petition based on your "feelings" or how hard you've worked. You cite the **Standard of Holiness** and the **Blood Covenant**. This is your "Legal ID", it proves you have the right to stand in the court and that your "Cargo" is insured by the highest power in the universe.

**The Writ of Mandamus:** In human law, a *Writ of Mandamus* is a "Command" issued by a higher court to a lower official or a "Gatekeeper," ordering them to do their job.

**The Spiritual Execution:** When you file this petition, you are serving a "Writ" to the demonic gatekeepers holding your finances, your health, or your "Star Deliverance." The Command is simple: **"Release the Cargo."** Because it is a Judicial Verdict, the gatekeeper has no choice. If they refuse, they are in "Contempt of Court," which brings the full "Veto Power" of heaven down upon their system.

## Recovering the "Cargo" with Precision

To make this "Deep and Strong," you must understand that this is a **Cargo Recovery Operation.**

**Identify the Goods:** During the Audit, you listed the "Missing Goods" (e.g., "I am missing 5 years of professional momentum").

**Locate the Vault:** You identify the "Illegal Merger", the place where you gave a system permission to siphon you (e.g., "I allowed this corporate system to own my innovation").

**Serve the Writ:** You use the language of the **Verdict**. You say: "By the Standard of Holiness, I rescind every illegal agreement. I demand a Writ of Mandamus against the Marine Siphons. You are ordered to return the Cargo, the years, the health, the wealth, and the joy, now."

This is how you move from "Flickering" back to being a **"Fixed Star."** You don't just "try harder." You audit the leak, identify the locust, and file the petition to bring your "Cargo" back to the surface. This is the legal foundation of your **Restoration.**

**The Scriptural Foundation** "Yet if he the thief, is caught, he must pay sevenfold; he may have to give up all the substance of his house." **Proverbs 6:31**

**The Verse Breakdown:**

**The Condition ("If he is caught"):** The "Audit" is how you catch the thief.

**The Sevenfold Penalty:** This is the **Judicial Multiplier**. You aren't just asking for the original "Cargo" back; you are legislating a penalty for the illegal siphoning.

**Total Asset Forfeiture:** The thief is legally required to empty his "house" (the Marine Vaults) to satisfy your petition.

## C. Breaking the "Ceiling of Ancestry"

Every leader faces a **Ceiling of Ancestry**, a specific legal height that no one in their bloodline has ever crossed. This is often the result of "Mother's Warnings" or "Foundational Corruption" that established a "cap" on the family's influence.

To break this ceiling, you must dismantle the **Specific Legal Barriers** (covenants, vows, or patterns of compromise) that acted as a "lid" on the previous generation. You are not just "doing better" than your parents; you are **annulling the law** that restricted them.

**The Deep Insight: The Judicial Ceiling**

If your ancestors formed "Illegal Mergers" or failed to "Model Righteousness," a legal precedent was set that says: *"No one from this bloodline can shine past this coordinate."* You break this by introducing the **Law of the Spirit of Life**, which has no ceiling.

**The Scriptural Foundation** "Christ has redeemed us from the curse of the law, having become a curse for us... that the blessing of Abraham might come upon the Gentiles..." , **Galatians 3:13-14**

**The Verse Breakdown:**

**The Legal Redemption:** Redemption is a **property term**. It means to "buy back" a deed. Christ bought back the deed to your bloodline.

**The Removal of the Limit:** By removing the "Curse of the Law" (the Ancestral Ceiling), you are legally reconnected to a higher "Bloodline", the blessing of Abraham.

**The Dimensional Shift:** You are no longer governed by your biological "floor"; you are now governed by a **Celestial Rank** that has no top.

## The Governor's Secret: Repossession is a Command

In this protocol, you are the **Bailiff of Heaven**. You are entering the enemy's territory to enforce a judgment that has already been signed by the King.

**Verdict:** The "Thieves of the Deep" rely on your ignorance of the Law. Once you file the petition, the "Marine Fogs" must clear, and the "Cargo" must be released. **The Gavel has fallen on your poverty, your sickness, and your delay.**

## Warfare prayer, chapter 7: the judicial protocols of recovery

**Target: Strategic Repossession & Ancestral Ceiling Destruction**

These prayers are **Writs of Execution**. In Chapter 7, you are not asking for a favor; you are acting as the **Celestial Bailiff** enforcing a court order for the immediate release of siphoned assets.

### Category I: The Divine Audit (Identifying the Leakage)

**1. The Decree of Exposure:**

"In my capacity as a Celestial Governor, I initiate a **Divine Audit** over my life. I command every hidden 'Foundational Crack' siphoning my health, my finances, and my joy to be exposed by the Light of the King. I identify every 'Illegal Merger' that has been quietly draining my virtue, and I mark it for immediate closure." **( Joel 2:25)**

**2. The Termination of Siphons:**

"I cite the 'Standard of Holiness' against every 'Marine Siphon' attached to my professional accounts and my peace of mind. I decree that the 'leakage' stops today. I legislatively sever every invisible cord connecting my 'Cargo' to the vaults of the night." **(Isaiah 10:27)**

### Category II: Filing the Celestial Petition (The Repossession)

**3. The Writ of Mandamus (Command to Release):**

"I file a **Celestial Petition** in the High Court of Heaven for the immediate return of my 'Prophetic Cargo.' I command the gates of the 'Deep' to open and vomit up my stolen time, my hijacked ideas, and my siphoned wealth. I refuse a partial return; I demand the full weight of my destiny's inventory." **( Job 20:15)**

**4. The Seven-Fold Multiplier:**

"I catch the 'Thief of the Deep' today! By the authority of **Proverbs 6:31**, I legislate a seven-fold penalty upon the systems that siphoned my virtue. I decree that the enemy must forfeit the 'substance of his house' to satisfy the debt owed to my bloodline. My recovery is multiplied!" **( Proverbs 6:31)**

**Category III: Breaking the "Ceiling of Ancestry" (The Floor-to-Ceiling Shift)**

**5. The Annulling of the Ancestral Lid:**

"I stand at the 'Coordinate of Truth' and I Veto the 'Ceiling of Ancestry' that stopped the leaders before me. I dismantle the specific legal barriers, the covenants of compromise and the 'Mother's Warnings', that acted as a lid on my family's influence. I declare that this ceiling is now my floor!" **(Galatians 3:13)**

**6. The Redrawing of the Bloodline Map:**

"I reject the 'biological limitations' of my lineage. I align myself with the **Bloodline of the Bright and Morning Star.** I decree that every generational delay that siphoned the time of my fathers is legally broken. I am moving into 'Noon-Day Authority' where no ancestral shadow can reach me." **( Hebrews 7:16)**

**Category IV: Recovering Marketplace Virtue (Industry Repossession)**

**7. The Repossession of Hijacked Ideas:**

"I decree a 'Judicial Recall' of every professional idea, business strategy, and creative spark that was siphoned by competitors or 'Star-Trackers.' I repossess my intellectual cargo from the vaults of the night and command it to manifest as tangible wealth in my hands." **(Isaiah 45:3)**

**8. The Restoration of Prophetic Time:**

"I command the 'Time-Sifters' to release the years they have eaten. I legislate a season of **Divine Acceleration** to compensate for every year spent in the 'Night Season' of confusion. I decree that I am catching up, taking over, and surpassing the coordinates of my original appointment." **( Amos 9:13)**

**Category V: Final Judicial Enforcement (The Gavel)**

**9. The Sealing of the Vaults:**

"I place a 'Celestial Seal' over my recovered assets. I forbid the 'Herod spirits' from re-tracking my progress. My finances are sanitized, my health is fortified, and my joy is untouchable. I am no longer a victim of systemic decay; I am the enforcer of Kingdom standards." **(Scripture: Ephesians 4:30)**

**10. The Final Gavel Fall:**

"The Gavel has fallen on the thieves of my destiny! My petition is granted, my cargo is released, and the ceiling is shattered. I arise in my **Repossessed Rank**, I shine with **Unleaked Power**, and I govern my estate with the absolute reliability of a Fixed Star. It is finished!" **(Isaiah 60:1)**

# Chapter 8: The No-Fly Zone

## Achieving Invisibility to Sabotage

In the life of a **Fixed Star**, visibility is a requirement for influence, but it is also a magnet for opposition. **The No-Fly Zone** is the strategic capacity to project immense light professionally while keeping your "Engine Room", your process, your source, and your next moves, completely invisible to those who operate in the frequency of sabotage.

## A. The Frequency of Silence: Hidden in Plain Sight

Many leaders believe they must be "loud" to be effective. However, true **Prophetic Governance** understands the power of the "Frequency of Silence." This is the ability to have your *work* highly visible and dominant in the marketplace while your *inner life* and *strategic blueprints* remain hidden.

**Public Output vs. Private Process:** Your "Star" should be seen, but the "Mapping" of its next orbit should be silent.

**The "Muffling" of the Ego:** Silence is a defensive frequency. When you stop broadcasting your personal details, you remove the "coordinates" that **Star-Trackers** use to calculate your vulnerability.

The **Frequency of Silence** is a specialized defensive protocol for leaders whose work is public but whose destiny is high-value. It is the art of being **strategically invisible** while remaining **operationally dominant**.

In this state, you operate like a stealth aircraft: you are carrying a massive payload (your innovation and cargo), and your "Star" is visible to the world, but your internal mechanics are completely off the radar of those who seek to track you.

## The Strategy of "Hidden in Plain Sight"

Most leaders make the mistake of believing that "Impact" equals "Access." They think that for their work to be loud, their lives must be loud. Prophetic Governance teaches the opposite.

**Public Output:** This is your "Star-Power" in action. It is the book, the business, the surgery, or the leadership. It should be bright, excellent, and undeniable in the marketplace.

**Private Process:** This is the "Mapping" of your next orbit. It includes your blueprints, your financial strategies, and your spiritual state. This must remain in a state of **Total Silence.**

**The Benefit:** By separating your *output* from your *process*, you give the "Human Systems" nothing to siphon and the "Herod Spirits" no target to strike. They can see what you *did*, but they can never see what you are *about to do*.

## The "Muffling" of the Ego: Removing the Coordinates

The greatest leak in a leader's life is often their own ego. The desire to be "known" or "validated" acts as a broadcast signal that trackers use to find you.

**Silence as a Shield:** When you broadcast your personal details, your struggles, or your "half-baked" ideas, you are essentially providing the **GPS coordinates** for the Herod Spirit. You are telling the "Tracking Systems" exactly where to find your "birth" center.

**Muffling the Signal:** By intentionally choosing silence, you "muffle" your frequency. You become a "ghost" in the system. The trackers may know you exist, but they cannot calculate your "Prophetic Rank" or your "trajectory" because you aren't giving them any data to work with.

## Star-Power without Exposure

True "Star Deliverance" means your light reaches its destination without you being consumed in the process.

**Operational Anonymity:** You can lead a global movement while keeping your inner circle and strategic blueprints behind a "Wall of Silence." This isn't about being secretive out of fear; it's about being **sacred** out of wisdom.

**The Power of the Unknown:** When a system doesn't know your next move, they cannot build a "Siphon" to catch it. Silence creates a "Lag Time" in the enemy's tracking, by the time they figure out your last move, you have already transitioned to a new "Prophetic Rank."

## The Deep Insight: The "Quiet" Throne

The higher the rank, the quieter the communication. In the celestial realm, the most powerful movements often happen in the "Third Heaven" silence. To protect your "Star Deliverance," you must learn to **broadcast the light, but bury the blueprint.**

**The Protocol:** If they can't track your frequency, they can't abort your legacy. Your effectiveness is not measured by how much people know *about* you, but by the weight of the "Cargo" you successfully deliver to the next generation.

**The Scriptural Foundation** "But when you do a charitable deed, do not let your left hand know what your right hand is doing, that your deed may be in secret; and your Father who sees in secret will Himself reward you openly.", Matthew **6:3-4**

**The Verse Breakdown:**

**The Internal Stealth:** This is a "No-Fly Zone" even within yourself. It's about cutting off the "frequency" of seeking human validation, which is often the entry point for "Herod Spirits."

**Secret Sowing, Open Reaping:** The legal result of silence is an **Open Reward**. When the process is hidden, the enemy cannot sabotage the harvest because they didn't know the seed was planted.

The principle of **Secret Sowing, Open Reaping** is the ultimate "counter-tracking" maneuver. In the legal framework of your legacy, silence isn't just about keeping a secret; it's about protecting the **integrity of the seed** until it has reached a level of maturity where it can no longer be "aborted" by the Herod Spirit or "siphoned" by corporate systems.

**How this works as a spiritual and professional law:**

**Denying the "Sabotage Window",** Every seed has a period of vulnerability, the time between when it is planted and when it takes root. This is the **Sabotage Window**.

**The Tracking Gap:** When you announce your plans prematurely (Public Sowing), you give the "Tracking Systems" time to calculate the exact location of your future harvest. They can then poison the soil, create a legal "Marine Fog" to confuse your direction, or plant "locusts" in the field before your crop even breaks the surface.

**The Power of the Stealth Seed:** By sowing in secret, you deny the enemy this window. Because they didn't see the "Seed" go into the ground, they haven't prepared a "Siphon" to catch the harvest. By the time they realize you have a "Star" rising, the harvest is already in your barn. You have achieved an **Open Reaping** because the defense was too late to react.

## The "Open Reward" as a Judicial Verdict

Scripturally and legally, there is a "Court Order" regarding silence: *He who sees in secret will reward you openly.* This is a **Celestial Guarantee.**

**The Undisputed Harvest:** When a reward is "Open," it means it is visible, undeniable, and legally yours. Because the "process" was hidden from the Siphons, they cannot claim "co-authorship" or "ownership" of the result.

**Avoiding the "Illegal Merger":** If a corporate system doesn't know you are developing a "Prophetic Cargo," they can't write a contract to seize it. Silence ensures that the "Reaping" belongs entirely to your own "Balance Sheet" rather than being drained into the "soot" of someone else's overhead.

## The "Maturity" Defense

The Herod Spirit tracks the "Birth" because that is when the vision is weakest. However, a "Star" that has already matured in silence is much harder to extinguish.

**Sudden Dominance:** When you reap openly after sowing secretly, you appear in the marketplace with **Full Strength**. You aren't a "baby" vision that can be aborted; you are a "Fixed Star" that has suddenly appeared in its full orbit.

**The Element of Surprise:** In the "Divine Audit" of your life, the most powerful assets are the ones the enemy didn't see coming. Your "Prophetic Rank" jumps significantly because you moved from "Seed" to "Harvest" without the trackers being able to log your progress.

## The Deep Insight: Protecting the "Genealogy" of the Idea

By keeping the seed secret, you protect the "DNA" of your innovation. You ensure that your legacy isn't "cross-pollinated" with the agendas of those who want to use you. The harvest is "Pure" because it grew in the **Frequency of Silence**, away from the noise and the siphons of the world.

**The Manuscript Protocol:** To sow in secret is to trust the Judge. To reap in the open is to demonstrate the Judge's Verdict.

## B. Strategic Sanitization: Cleaning the Environment

Every interaction in the "Night Season" leaves a residue, what we call **Spiritual Soot**. Whether it is digital (social media monitoring) or physical (toxic workplace atmospheres), this soot creates a "film" over your star, making it "flicker" and making you "trackable."

**Digital Sanitization:** Removing yourself from "Illegal Mergers" online and closing the digital gateways that allow "Star-Hunters" to peer into your life.

**Physical Sanitization:** Cleansing your physical office and home from the "frequency of envy" and the "smog of compromise."

**The Scriptural Foundation,** "Therefore, 'Come out from among them and be separate," says the Lord. Do not touch what is unclean, and I will receive you.', 2 **Corinthians 6:17**

**The Verse Breakdown:**

**The Separation Mandate:** Sanitization is a **Judicial Requirement** for receiving the full weight of Kingdom authority.

**The "Unclean" Frequency:** "Unclean" refers to anything that carries the soot of the "Prince of this world." By separating your frequency, you move into a higher jurisdiction where you are "received" (protected and authorized).

## C. Neutralizing Monitoring Spirits: Stealth Mode

**Monitoring Spirits** are the "surveillance drones" of the spirit realm. They don't always attack; they simply *watch* to see when you are about to launch a major project or enter a new "Rank." **Stealth Mode** is the judicial protocol of "scrambling" their signals so you can execute your mandate without alerting competitors or the "Herod Entity."

**Scrambling the Signal:** Using your authority to decree **"Judicial Blindness"** over those who track your progress with evil intent.

**Executing in the "Secret Place":** Building your "Kingdom Estate" in a way that the world only sees the finished product, never the "scaffolding" where you are vulnerable.

**The Scriptural Foundation** "He who dwells in the secret place of the Most High shall abide under the shadow of the Almighty.", Psalm **91:1**

**The Verse Breakdown:**

**The Secret Place:** This is the ultimate **No-Fly Zone**. It is a coordinate that is "unmappable" by any demonic monitoring system.

**The Shadow Override:** When you dwell here, you are covered by a "Shadow" (The Almighty) that is infinitely darker and more powerful than the "Night Season." It acts as a "Cloaking Device" for your destiny.

## The Governor's Secret: Visibility is for Results, Stealth is for Strategy

A "Star" that is always explaining itself is a star that is easily caught. To achieve **Fixed Star** status, you must learn to move in the "No-Fly Zone", where your results are undeniable, but your "how" is a mystery to the night.

**Verdict:** The enemy cannot hit what he cannot see. By sanitizing your space and embracing the frequency of silence, you ensure that the only thing the world sees is your **Glow**, never your **Map**.

## Warfare prayer, chapter 8: the no-fly zone

### Target: Strategic Invisibility & Environmental Sanitization

These prayers are **Cloaking Decrees**. In Chapter 8, you are legislating a "Stealth Protocol" that allows your influence to rise while keeping your process unmappable. Pray these to scramble the sonar of every "Star-Hunter" and monitoring system.

### Category I: The Frequency of Silence (The Cloaking Device)

**1. The Decree of Interior Stealth:**

"In the name of the Lord, I activate the **Frequency of Silence** over my inner blueprints. I decree that my 'Right Hand' shall move in such high-level secrecy that my 'Left Hand', and every external observer, cannot track the coordinate of my next move. I muzzle the frequency of self-validation and cloth myself in the invisibility of the King." **(Matthew 6:3-4)**

**2. The Muffling of Personal Data:**

"I withdraw my personal coordinates from the 'Night Season's' database. I decree that my private life, my vulnerabilities, and my strategic 'Engine Room' are now off-limits to public surveillance. I am visible for my fruit, but hidden in my root." **(Colossians 3:3)**

### Category II: Strategic Sanitization (The Environmental Cleanse)

**3. The Digital Fire-Wall:**

"I legislatively 'Sanitize' my digital and physical spaces. I command every residue of 'Spiritual Soot', envy, monitoring, and siphoning, to be incinerated by the Fire of the Spirit. I close every digital gateway that has allowed 'Star-Trackers' to peer into my Kingdom Estate. My environment is now a **Sanctified Zone." (2 Corinthians 6:17)**

**4. The Eviction of the Herod-Spirit:**

"I identify every 'Herod-spirit' lurking in my professional and social circles under the guise of 'interest' or 'mentorship.' I decree an immediate judicial eviction. I cleanse my atmosphere from the frequency of betrayal and the smog of compromise. Only those aligned with the **Standard of Holiness** have the legal right to remain in my orbit." **(Psalm 101:7)**

**Category III: Neutralizing Monitoring Spirits (Scrambling the Signal)**

**5. The Decree of Judicial Blindness:**

"I invoke **Judicial Blindness** upon every 'Monitoring Spirit' assigned to track my progress. I scramble their spiritual sonar and confuse their tracking signals. I decree that when they look for me, they shall see only the 'Shadow of the Almighty,' and not the coordinate of my person." **(2 Kings 6:18)**

**6. The Scrambling of Competitive Surveillance:**

"I command a 'Prophetic Scramble' over the intelligence systems of my competitors and detractors. I decree that every attempt to calculate my 'Prophetic Rank' or siphoning my marketplace strategies shall end in total confusion. My moves are executed in **Stealth Mode**, untouchable by the night." **(Job 5:12-13)**

**Category IV: Establishing the No-Fly Zone (The Airspace Protection)**

**7. The Legislative Airspace Closure:**

"I establish a permanent **No-Fly Zone** over my household, my children, and my visionary projects. I forbid every 'High-Altitude' principality from hovering over my decision making process. My atmosphere is high pressure and Kingdom saturated, unfit for the flight of any demonic drone." **(Psalm 91:10)**

**8. The Cloaking of the Seed Bank:**

"I decree that the 'Seed-Bank' of my future projects is now hidden in the **Secret Place.** I legislate that my ideas shall incubate in total silence until they are ready for a 'High-Noon' manifestation. I refuse to broadcast my 'pregnancy' until the day of birth!" **(Psalm 27:5)**

**Category V: Final Judicial Sealing (The Gavel)**

**9. The Decree of the Moving Target:**

"I refuse to be a predictable, 'trackable' leader. I move by the **GPS of the Spirit**, re-routing my path whenever the 'Herod Entity' attempts a lock. I am a moving target in the spirit—always ten steps ahead of the 'Star-Hunters' and always perfectly aligned with the King's timing." **(Matthew 2:12)**

**10. The Gavel Falls on Sabotage:**

"The Gavel has fallen! The 'No-Fly Zone' is active. My sanitization is complete, my stealth is absolute, and my influence is unstoppable. I move in the **Shadow of the Almighty**, invisible to sabotage but dominant in the marketplace. It is finished!" **(Psalm 91:1)**

# Chapter 9: The Governor's Veto Power

## Enforcing Kingdom Standards in Secular Systems

To exercise the **Veto** is to move from being a victim of your environment to being the **Chief Executive** of your own existence. In the framework of "Star Deliverance," your life, your home, and your business are not just "spaces", they are **Sovereign Kingdom Estates.** A Veto is a high-level judicial act. It is the power to say "No" to a law, a culture, or a frequency that is seeking to govern your territory.

## A. Exercising the Veto: Blocking Toxic Culture

### Spiritual Border Control: Protecting the Threshold

Just as a nation-state has a border to protect its citizens and its economy, a leader with a "Prophetic Rank" must maintain a **Spiritual Border.**

**The Frequencies of Entry:** Toxic culture, whether it's the "Smog of Compromise" in a corporate office or the "Marine Fogs" of modern secularism, is constantly looking for a port of entry. It wants to cross the threshold of your influence to "muffle" your Star.

**The Act of Blocking:** You must act as your own "Border Control." This means recognizing frequencies like **rebellion, perversion, or mediocrity** as "illegal aliens" in your estate. You don't "negotiate" with mediocrity; you Veto its entry. You refuse to let it settle in your thoughts, your staff, or your family culture.

### The Refusal of the Signature: Breaking the Illegal Merger

In the "Human Systems" of the corporate world, there is often an unwritten rule: *To rise to the top, you must sign off on our decay.* They ask you to "model" their lack of integrity or their

"Foundational Corruption" as a price for your "Star-Power" to be seen.

**The Silent Consent:** If you remain silent while a system siphons your virtue or compromises your standards, you are "signing that system into law" for your life. Your silence is your signature.

**The Sovereign Refusal:** Exercising the Veto means you **refuse to sign.** You recognize that your success does not depend on their "decayed" infrastructure. By saying "No" to their compromise, you are declaring that your **Standard of Holiness** is not a religious limitation, it is a **Superior Technology**. It is the very thing that keeps your Star "Fixed" while theirs eventually burns out.

## Policing the "Estate"

Once the Veto is exercised, you must maintain the "State of the Estate." This involves a constant "Divine Audit" of the atmosphere you allow around you.

**The Smog of Compromise:** This is a slow-moving "locust" that tries to dim your light by making you "just like everyone else." The Veto clears the air.

**The Marine Fog:** This is the confusion that tries to make you forget your "Constitutional Appointment." The Veto acts as a spiritual "wind" that pushes the fog back to the sea, allowing you to see your "Cargo" clearly again.

## The Deep Insight: The Veto as Deliverance

The Veto is the tool you use to "Rescind" the agreements you made in the "Night Season" of your life. It is the moment you decide that your "Star" will no longer be a tenant in a toxic system.

When you Veto a toxic culture, you aren't just "quitting" or "complaining", you are **legally disconnecting** your energy from their "Siphon." You are reclaiming your sovereignty so that when the "Open Reaping" comes, it isn't contaminated by the soot of their system.

**The Leader's Decree:** "I do not belong to the system I am changing. I exercise my Veto over every frequency of compromise, and I sign into law the Standard of Holiness over my Estate."

**The Scriptural Foundation,** "I will set nothing wicked before my eyes; I hate the work of those who fall away; it shall not cling to me." **Psalm 101:3**

**The Verse Breakdown:**

**The Executive Decision:** "I will set nothing..." is a Veto. It is a refusal to allow a specific frequency to enter the visual or mental gateway.

**The Prevention of Clinging:** The Veto ensures that the "Soot" of the world does not have the legal "cling" required to track your star or siphoning your virtue.

## B. Legislative Decrees: Beyond "Asking" to "Decreeing"

Most people spend their lives "asking" the atmosphere for permission to succeed. A Governor moves into **Legislative Decrees**. This is the shift from petitioning (asking for a favor) to legislating (declaring a standard). When you decree, you are setting a new "Coordinate of Truth" that the environment must align with.

**Setting the Standard:** Instead of asking for a promotion, you decree a standard of excellence that makes your promotion a **Judicial Necessity**.

**Atmospheric Legislation:** You move into your workplace and decree: "In this coordinate, integrity is the law. Deception is unconstitutional."

**The Scriptural Foundation,** "You will also declare a thing, and it will be established for you; so light will shine on your ways.", Job **22:28**

**The Verse Breakdown:**

**The Act of Declaration:** This is a legislative act. It is not a suggestion; it is a **Statute**.

**The Establishment:** The word "established" implies a "fixed" state. Once you decree it, the environment becomes a "Fixed Star" around your word.

**The Resulting Light:** The light shines because the Veto has cleared the "Marine Fogs" that previously caused confusion.

## C. The Throne Room Connection: Operating from Rest

The ultimate secret of the Governor is the **Throne Room Connection**. You do not exercise power by "striving" or "fighting" in the trenches. You operate from a **Seated Position**. This is the position of **Rest**, where you realize that your authority is not based on your effort, but on your **Prophetic Rank**.

**Seated Authority:** While your influence is out "working", managing teams, closing deals, and protecting your children, your spirit remains "seated" in a state of absolute reliability and peace.

**The Rest Factor:** The enemy cannot "muffle" a leader who is at rest. Anxiety is a "Flickering" frequency; Rest is the frequency of a **Fixed Star**.

**The Scriptural Foundation,** "...and raised us up together, and made us sit together in the heavenly places in Christ Jesus.", **Ephesians 2:6**

**The Verse Breakdown:**

**The Judicial Seat:** You are not standing, running, or begging. You are **Seated**.

**The High Noon Coordinate:** "Heavenly places" is the highest possible coordinate. From this rank, every "Prince" and "Herod-spirit" is beneath your feet.

**The Collaborative Governance:** "Together with Him" means your Veto carries the weight of the King's Gavel.

## The Governor's Secret: The Veto is Immediate

A Veto does not take years to manifest; it is a change in **Legal Status** the moment it is issued. When you decide that "Systemic Decay" is no longer the law in your house, the atmosphere must immediately begin the process of eviction.

**Verdict:** You have been appointed to govern, not to negotiate with darkness. Drop the Gavel of your Veto and watch the secular systems bow to the **Standard of Holiness**.

**Now, the question is; Is there a culture in your sphere that needs to be Vetoed today?**

## Warfare prayer, chapter 9: the governor's veto power

### Target: The Executive Veto & Throne Room Governance

These prayers are **Legislative Instruments**. In Chapter 9, you are no longer a petitioner; you are the **Governor** of your jurisdiction. Pray these to override secular decay and enforce the King's Standard over your business, home, and bloodline.

**Category I: Exercising the Veto (The Border Closure)**

**1. The Veto of Toxic Frequencies:**

"By my authority as a Celestial Governor, I exercise my **Executive Veto** against the entry of toxic culture into my Kingdom Estate. I forbid the 'Smog of Compromise,' the spirit of rebellion, and the frequency of mediocrity from being signed into law in my home or business. I decree a permanent border closure against systemic decay." **(Psalm 101:3)**

**2. The Refusal of Secular Signatures:**

"I refuse to sign my name or my 'Star' to any agreement that requires the siphoning of my integrity. I Veto every 'Illegal Merger' proposed by secular systems that seek to muffle my light. I declare that the **Standard of Holiness** is the only law recognized in this coordinate." **( 2 Corinthians 6:14)**

**Category II: Legislative Decrees (The New Statute)**

**3. The Decree of Industry Excellence:**

"I move beyond asking for favor to **Decreeing a New Standard.** I legislate a statute of 'Incorruptible Excellence' over my professional sphere. I decree that every project I touch must align with the 'Coordinate of Truth.' I set the pace; I do not follow the 'Marine Fogs' of industry trends." **( Job 22:28)**

**4. The Override of Stagnation:**

"I legislate an immediate 'Override' against the spirit of stagnation in my family and finance. I decree a new law of **Perpetual Acceleration.** I command every gatekeeper of 'Status Quo' to step aside, for a higher Decree has been issued from the Throne Room." **(Scripture: Isaiah 43:19)**

**Category III: The Throne Room Connection (The Seated Rank)**

**5. The Enforcement of Seated Rest:**

"I take my seat in the **Heavenly Places,** far above every 'Prince' and 'Herod-spirit.' I decree that I shall not govern from a place of striving, but from a position of absolute **Rest.** I command my influence to work on my behalf while I remain centered in the King's peace." **(Ephesians 2:6)**

**6. The Scrambling of Opposition from the Height:**

"From my seated rank, I look down upon every 'Star-Hunter' and monitoring system. I decree that their calculations are irrelevant because they cannot map a frequency that originates from the Throne. I am governed by a Law they cannot comprehend and a Rank they cannot veto." **(Psalm 2:4)**

**Category IV: Enforcing Kingdom Standards (The Market Override)**

**7. The Judicial Sanitization of the Workplace:**

"I decree that my workplace is now a **Sanctified Zone.** I Veto the 'Normalized Evils' of gossip, deception, and theft. I legislate that the 'Kavod' (Weight) of God's Presence shall be the primary atmosphere in my boardroom. Those who cannot align with this frequency must legally vacate the premises." **( Psalm 101:7)**

**8. The Veto of Generational Leaks:**

"I Veto the 'Generational Leak' that siphoned the virtue of the leaders before me. I decree that the 'Foundational Corruption' of my ancestry has no legal standing in my current jurisdiction. I am a **New Bloodline Standard,** and I enforce the Law of the Spirit of Life over my children's future." **( Romans 8:2)**

**Category V: Final Executive Enforcement (The Gavel)**

**9. The Decree of the Infallible Gavel:**

"I drop the **Gavel of the Spirit** over my city and my industry. I decree that my Veto is immediate and irreversible. Every demonic drone and monitoring spirit is hereby grounded. The 'Night Season' must bow to the 'Noon-Day Authority' of the Governor." **(Matthew 18:18)**

**10. The Final Activation of the Governor:**

"The Gavel has fallen! I am no longer negotiating; I am legislating. I arise in my **Throne Room Connection,** I shine with **Veto Power,** and I govern my territory with the reliability of a Fixed Star. The Standard of Holiness is enforced, and my Kingdom Estate is secure. It is finished!" **(Isaiah 60:1)**

# Chapter 10: Legacy Wealth & the Eternal Rank

## Securing the Future of the Bloodline

The final chapter of **Star Deliverance** moves from your personal governance to the establishment of an eternal dynasty. In this stage, you are no longer just a leader; you are a **Foundational Ancestor**. You are moving beyond your own lifespan to ensure that your "Star" becomes a permanent fixture in the history of your bloodline and your industry.

## A. The Seed-Bank Strategy: Children as Constitutional Assets

Most parents view their children's future as a "family hope", something they wish for or pray about. A **Celestial Governor** views their children's potential as a **Constitutional Asset**. This is the "Seed-Bank Strategy." You are the guardian of a divine deposit that belongs to the Kingdom's economy.

**Asset Protection:** You do not leave your children's potential "unprotected" in the open market of the world. You wrap their destiny in a **Judicial Trust** of prayer, character, and excellence.

**The Legislative Hedge:** You decree that their potential is "Sovereign Property." This prevents **Star-Trackers** from identifying them as "prey" and ensures that their "virtue" cannot be siphoned by toxic peers or systems.

This shift in perspective moves parenting from the realm of **sentimental hope** to **strategic governance**. When you view your child's potential as a **Constitutional Asset**, you are treating them as a high-value resource that has been "deposited" into your care.

In this "Seed-Bank Strategy," you aren't just raising a child; you are managing a **Divine Investment** that must be protected from the "Tracking Systems" we discussed earlier.

## Asset Protection: The Judicial Trust

In the financial world, an asset that is left in the "open market" is vulnerable to every predator and market crash. A Celestial Governor understands that a child's destiny must be "wrapped" in a **Judicial Trust** to keep it out of reach from those who would exploit it.

**The Protection Wrap:** This trust is built from three materials: **Prayer (Spiritual), Character (Moral), and Excellence (Professional).** When you wrap a child in these, you are creating a legal shield.

**Beyond the Reach of Siphons:** By the time the world (the "open market") tries to put its hooks into your child, they find that the child's potential is already "assigned." The "Corporate Siphons" cannot claim ownership of their ideas, and the "Herod Spirits" cannot find an entry point, because the child's identity is already "legally bound" to a higher system of integrity.

## The Legislative Hedge: Declaring Sovereign Property

A "Hedge" is not a wall of fear; it is a **Jurisdictional Boundary.** By declaring your child's potential as **Sovereign Property**, you are moving them from the "Public Domain" (where anyone can influence or track them) to a "Private Kingdom Estate."

**Blocking the Star-Trackers:** The "Herod Spirits" track stars at their birth. By legislating a hedge around your children, you are essentially "cloaking" their prophetic rank. You are saying to the trackers: *"This asset is not for sale, and it is not prey. It is protected by the Standard of Holiness."*

**The Prevention of Virtue Drainage:** Children often experience "Virtue Leakage" through toxic peers, media, or educational systems that aim to "muffle" their frequency. The Legislative Hedge acts as a **Frequency Filter.** It allows the child to be *in* the world but ensures that the world's "soot" cannot settle on their potential.

## The Deep Strategy: The Seed-Bank

A seed bank exists to ensure that even if the world experiences a "Night Season" or a famine, the **pure DNA** of the future is preserved.

**The Guardian's Duty:** As the Governor of this Seed-Bank, your job is to ensure the "DNA" of your child's purpose remains uncorrupted. You are protecting the "Mantle" before it is ever worn.

**Preventing the Illegal Merger:** Many children are "merged" into toxic systems (like debt, addiction, or mediocrity) before they even reach adulthood. Your governance ensures that no "Illegal Mergers" are signed into law during their minority. You keep their "Balance Sheet" clean until they are strong enough to exercise their own **Veto Power.**

## The Deep Insight: The Parental Verdict

You aren't just "wishing" for their success; you are **signing their future into law.** When you govern your children this way, you are acting as the **Guardian of Destiny.** You are ensuring that when they step into their "Star-Power," they do so with a full tank of virtue, an untouched cargo of potential, and no "Marine Fogs" Clouding their vision.

**The Decree:** "My children are Constitutional Assets of the Kingdom. Their potential is Sovereign Property. Every 'Herod Spirit' is Vetoed from their timeline, and every 'Siphon' is blocked from their virtue. They are Fixed Stars in the making."

**The Scriptural Foundation**, "A good man leaves an inheritance to his children's children, but the wealth of the sinner is stored up for the righteous.", Proverbs 13:22

**The Verse Breakdown:**

**The Multi-Generational Scope:** The inheritance is not just for the next generation, but the one after. This is **Eternal Ranking**.

**The Asset Transfer:** The "wealth of the sinner" (the siphoned virtue of the world) is legislatively redirected to the "Seed-Bank" of the righteous.

I pray for you in the name of Jesus, let there be wealthy transfer from the hands of the unrighteous to the hands of the children of God.

## B. Establishing the Star-Standard: Ceiling to Floor

The "Star-Standard" is the blueprint you leave behind so that your children never have to repeat your "Night Seasons." The goal of a Governor is to ensure that your **Ceiling** (your highest point of achievement and spiritual rank) becomes their **Floor** (their starting point).

**The Blueprint of Excellence:** You document the "Coordinate of Truth" so they don't have to spend forty years "mapping" the territory you have already conquered.

**Annulling the Reset:** Many families "reset" to zero every generation because of **Foundational Corruption.** You break that cycle by establishing a **Star-Standard** of integrity that remains constant even after you have transitioned.

The **Star-Standard** is the ultimate act of generational architecture. In most families, success is a "revolving door", one generation rises, only for the next to fall back to zero because the "Foundational Corruption" was never cleared. This is the "Night Season" cycle, where each child has to rediscover the light for themselves.

A Celestial Governor ends this cycle. You do not just leave behind an inheritance of money; you leave behind an inheritance of **Position**.

## The Physics of the Floor: Converting Victory into Foundation

The "Ceiling to Floor" principle is about **Spiritual and Professional Leverage**. If you spent forty years fighting "Marine Siphons" and clearing the "Soot" of your industry to reach a high rank, that victory is a waste if your children have to fight those same battles from scratch.

**The Transfer of Rank:** By establishing the Star-Standard, you are legally transferring your "Prophetic Rank" to them. You are saying that the territory you conquered is now "Secured Land."

**Starting at the Summit:** When your highest point (your Ceiling) becomes their starting point (their Floor), they don't have to spend their youth "mapping" the wilderness. They begin their journey already standing on the heights you bled to reach. Their energy isn't wasted on survival; it is invested entirely in **Expansion**.

## The Blueprint of Excellence: The Coordinates of Truth

Most families lose their way because they don't leave a "map." They leave "wishes," but not "blueprints."

**The Strategic Map:** Documenting the **Coordinate of Truth** means you are giving your children the "GPS coordinates" of how you succeeded. You are explaining exactly how you exercised the Veto, how you filed the Petition, and how you maintained the Frequency of Silence.

**Removing the Guesswork:** When the blueprint is clear, the "Star-Trackers" cannot deceive your children. Your children will recognize a "Herod Spirit" or a "Siphon" immediately because you have already identified its "signature" in the family ledger.

## Annulling the Reset: Breaking the Cycle of Corruption

The "Reset" happens when a family has a **Foundational Crack**. Maybe the parents achieved success but did so through compromise, leaving a "debt" of integrity that the children eventually have to pay.

**Breaking the "Zero" Trap:** Many dynasties "reset to zero" every thirty years because they didn't have a Star-Standard of integrity. They had wealth, but they didn't have a **Standard of Holiness**.

**The Constant Light:** By establishing a standard that remains constant even after you have transitioned, you ensure the family "Star" never sets. You are building a system of integrity that is so strong it functions as a **Perpetual Motion Machine**. Even in your absence, the "Floor" remains solid because it is built on the Judicial Verdicts you signed into law while you were seated on the Throne.

## The Deep Insight: The Legacy of Momentum

This is how you build a **"Kingdom Dynasty."** You aren't just passing down assets; you are passing down **Momentum**.

When a child starts at your Ceiling, they aren't just "richer" or "smarter", they are **farther along the path of destiny**. They can see things you couldn't see because they are standing on your shoulders. Your "Star Deliverance" wasn't just for you; it was to ensure that they would never know the "Night Season" that nearly consumed you.

**The Governor's Legacy:** "I am not just raising a child; I am building a Floor. I am documenting the path so they can run where I had to crawl. My Ceiling is their starting line, and their Star will never have to fight for the ground I have already won."

**The Scriptural Foundation,** "I will not hide them from their children, telling to the generation to come the praises of the Lord... that the generation to come might know them, the children who would be born, that they may arise and declare them to their children.", **Psalm 78:4-6**

**The Verse Breakdown:**

**The Chain of Command:** This is the legislative transmission of the "Star-Standard."

**The Arising:** Notice the command to "Arise." This is the same frequency as "Arise, Shine." It ensures that the next generation doesn't stay in the "Night Season" but starts in the light you provided.

## C. The Final Activation: From Luminance to Fixed Star

In this final protocol, you move from being a "Luminance of Interest" someone who is currently shining to a **Fixed Star of History**, someone whose influence is permanent. This is your **Judicial Commission**. It is the moment where your work is "Sanitized" from the temporary and sealed into the eternal.

**Fixed Position:** A "Fixed Star" does not move, fade, or flicker. It becomes a **Navigational Point** for everyone else in the industry.

**The Eternal Rank:** You are commissioned into a rank where your name and your work continue to "Veto" darkness in your industry long after your hands have left the plow.

**The Scriptural Foundation,** "Those who are wise shall shine like the brightness of the firmament, and those who turn many to righteousness like the stars forever and ever.", **Daniel 12:3**

**The Verse Breakdown:**

**The Requirement of Wisdom:** The "Mapping" and "Strategy" you have learned throughout this book are what secure this rank.

**The Duration:** "Forever and ever." This is the transition from a seasonal appointment to an **Eternal Rank.**

**The Global Influence:** Turning "many to righteousness" means your "Star" has become a coordinate for the masses to find their way out of the "Marine Fogs" and into the light.

## The Governor's Final Word: It is Settled

You started as a leader looking for purpose. You end as a **Fixed Star** governing the future. Your bloodline is secure, your "Cargo" has been repossessed, and your "Veto Power" is absolute.

**Verdict:** The "Night Season" has no more power over you. You have been commissioned. You have been Sanitized and your Star is now a permanent law in the firmament of leadership.

**The Gavel has fallen. Arise and Shine.**

# Warfare prayer, chapter 10: legacy wealth & the eternal rank

### Target: Bloodline Security & Eternal Ranking

These final prayers are **Covenant Seals**. In Chapter 10, you are legislating the permanent protection of your legacy. You are moving from daily warfare to the establishment of an **Eternal Dynasty** that cannot be moved or siphoned by time.

### Category I: The Seed-Bank Strategy (Asset Protection)

### 1. The Constitutional Trust Decree:

"I place the potential of my children into a **Celestial Trust.** I decree that their gifts, their health, and their 'Star-Power' are **Constitutional Assets** of the Kingdom. I forbid the 'Star-Hunters' and 'Marine Siphons' from accessing their life-inventory. My seed is protected by the highest Law in the firmament." **(Proverbs 13:22)**

**2. The Hedge of Invisibility:**

"I establish a 'Hedge of Fire' around the 'Seed-Bank' of my future generations. I decree that my children are unmappable to the systems of the night. I Veto every cultural influence designed to steal their virtue, and I declare their destiny is a **Sovereign Kingdom Estate.**" **(Job 1:10)**

**Category II: The Star-Standard (Ceiling-to-Floor Shift)**

**3. The Blueprint of Continuity:**

"I decree that the 'Night Seasons' of my past shall never be repeated by my children. I legislatively establish my **Ceiling as their Floor.** I release the 'Star-Standard' of excellence and integrity into their DNA, ensuring that they start their journey at my highest coordinate of victory." **(Psalm 78:4-6)**

**4. The Annulment of the 'Reset' Spirit:**

"I dismantle the spirit of 'Foundational Corruption' that causes families to reset to zero. I decree that my bloodline is a **Continuous Orbit.** We shall not go backward; we shall move from 'Rank to Rank' and 'Light to Light' until the perfect day." **(Proverbs 4:18)**

**Category III: Legacy Wealth (Repossessing the Future)**

**5. The Redirection of Siphoned Wealth:**

"I cite **Proverbs 13:22** and I command the wealth of the 'Night Season' to be legislatively redirected into my family's Seed-Bank. I decree that the resources siphoned from my ancestors are now being returned to fund the 'Prophetic Mandate' of my children's children." **(Isaiah 61:6-7)**

**6. The Inheritance of the Bright Star:**

"I decree that my children are the 'Rightful Heirs' of marketplace dominance. I forbid them from being 'borrowers' or 'servants' to the systems of the world. They are the **Lenders to Nations**, carrying the frequency of the 'Fixed Star' into every economy they enter." **(Deuteronomy 28:12)**

**Category IV: The Final Activation (Luminance to Fixed Star)**

**7. The Commission of the Fixed Star:**

"I move from being a 'Luminance of Interest' to a **Fixed Star of History.** I decree that my work, my book, and my name are now sealed into the 'Firmament of Leadership.' I shall not fade, I shall not flicker, and my influence shall outlive my natural breath." **(Daniel 12:3)**

**8. The Navigation Coordinate:**

"I decree that my life is now a **Navigational Point** for those lost in the 'Marine Fogs.' I take my seat as a Foundational Ancestor of Integrity. Every person who reads my words or follows my path is legally protected from the 'Star-Trackers' of their own generation." **(Matthew 5:14)**

**Category V: The Eternal Gavel Fall (The Final Seal)**

**9. The Sealing of the Bloodline Gate:**

"I place the **Standard of Holiness** over the gates of my bloodline for the next ten generations. I decree that no 'Prince of Darkness' has the jurisdiction to enter my house again. The 'Gavel of the Spirit' has fallen on my family's past, and the future is a **Coordinate of Truth." (Isaiah 54:17)**

**10. The Final Execution of Rank:**

"The Gavel has fallen! The manual is complete. I arise as, a Fixed Star, a Celestial Governor, and a Guardian of Destiny. My rank is eternal, my seed is secure, and my light is absolute. **IT IS FINISHED!" (Revelation 22:16)**

# CONCLUSION:

The decree has been issued, the protocols have been established, and the atmosphere around your destiny has been sanitized. You are no longer a "flickering candle" at the mercy of the wind; you are a **Celestial Governor** locked into your legal Prophetic Rank.

As you close this manual, remember that **Preservation** is an ongoing legislative act. The kingdom of darkness does not retreat because of a single prayer; it retreats because of a **Persistent Shine.** You must maintain your "Seat at the Gate" with the same ferocity with which you recovered it.

## THE FINAL STANDING ORDER

**Keep the Lens Clean:** Never allow the "Smog of Compromise" to settle. Live a life of high-frequency integrity so that the King's light can pass through you without distortion.

**Enforce the No-Fly Zone:** Be vigilant over your household. Use the Blood of the Lamb to scrub the air and keep your children's stars hidden in the "Secret Place" from every spiritual telescope.

**Navigate with Excellence:** Do not just work; **Govern.** Let your transactions be so transparent and your results so undeniable that the "Kings of the Earth" have no choice but to track the coordinate of your light.

Governor, the "Night Season" of your life is over. Even if the world remains in darkness, you are now operating from the frequency of the **Noon-Day Sun.** You are the "City on a Hill." You are the "Bethlehem Signal." You are the "Mother of Lions" guarding the stars of the next generation.

Go forth and occupy your orbit. The firmament of your industry, your family, and your territory is waiting for the impact of your rising. The Gavel has fallen in your favor, and the verdict is absolute: **You shall not dim, you shall not fall, and you shall not be displaced.**

**The night belongs to the Lord, and the stars belong to Zion.**

**About the Author - Dr. Philomena Gerald**
**Medical Doctor | Intercessor | Author | Kingdom Strategist**

Dr. Philomena Gerald is a medical doctor, devoted wife and mother, and a commissioned intercessor with a global mandate for spiritual restoration and deliverance. She is the Founder and visionary leader of *Jesus Deliverance Clinic International Ministries*, a dynamic apostolic hub dedicated to healing, foundational reconstruction, and the enforcement of Kingdom authority.

With a rare integration of medical expertise and deep spiritual insight, Dr. Philomena operates at the intersection of clinical care and spiritual deliverance, addressing both physical conditions and foundational spiritual issues affecting individuals, families, and communities.

## Calling & Ministry Assignment

Dr. Philomena is widely recognized as the Convener of the *Midnight Battle Intercessory Prayer*, a strategic and prophetic movement that mobilizes believers to engage in targeted spiritual warfare. This platform emphasizes the execution of divine judgments, referred to as the **"Verdict of the Decree"**, against entrenched powers of darkness.

Her ministry assignment centers on:

- Restoring broken foundations
- Uprooting generational patterns and legal claims
- Equipping believers to function as Governors of Light
- Enforcing Kingdom laws through spiritual intelligence and prayer

**Her mission is clear:**
To transition the Body of Christ from subjects of circumstance into rulers of spiritual territory through deep foundational deliverance.

# The Library of Dr. Philomena Gerald

Strategies for Governance, Deliverance, and Kingdom Authority

Featured Publications

1. Deep Foundational Deliverance
   Judicial Focus: Secret to Spiritual Warfare: Identifying and uprooting hidden legal claims and ancient cycles of defeat.
2. Prayer Against Witchcraft: Overruled
   Judicial Focus: Dismantling Darkness: Severe warfare and judicial decrees to break foundations of sorcery and demonic monitoring.
3. Deliverance from Addiction
   Judicial Focus: Restoring the Temple: Judicial prayers to break mental disorders, wasting spirits, and the cycle of premature death.
4. Courts of Heaven (Vol. 1): From Defendant to Ruler
   Judicial Focus: The Governor's Brief: Moving from a victim of circumstance to a ruler of spiritual territory through legal protocol.
5. Courts of Heaven (Vol. 2): Silencing the Accuser
   Judicial Focus: Securing the Verdict: A tactical guide to winning spiritual battles by enforcing the final judgments of the King.
6. Children Daily Prayer Manual
   Judicial Focus: The Next Generation: A 365-day training protocol for commissioning Kingdom Executives and Royal Governors.
7. Praying Mother – Gatekeepers Womb
   Judicial Focus: The "Touch Not" Mandate: A Mother's Manual for Family Deliverance and the Preservation of Thrones.

8. Sex Before Marriage – Foundational Corruption
   Judicial Focus: The Stewardship of the Body, the Mystery of Illegal Covenants, and the Mandate for a New Blood line.
9. Deliverance from Marine Kingdom
   Judicial Focus: Exposing the Marine Kingdom's Hidden Infrastructure: From Underwater Banks to Biological Laboratories.
10. Star Deliverance
   Judicial Focus: A Divine Manual for Protecting Your Prophetic Rank and Reclaiming Your Destiny from Spiritual Thieves.

## Where to Locate & Listen

1. E-Books & Paperbacks: Available on Google Books, Amazon Kindle, and Barnes & Noble.
2. Audiobooks: Professionally narrated versions are available on Apple Books, Audible, and ACX.
3. Audio Streaming: Search for "Dr. Philomena Gerald" on your preferred audiobook provider to listen on the go.

## About the Ministry

1. Dr. Philomena Gerald is a commissioned voice for the restoration of foundations and the enforcement of Kingdom Law.
2. Primary Ministry: Founder of Jesus Deliverance Clinic International Ministries, a global hub for spiritual healing and foundational reconstruction.
3. The Midnight Call: Convener of the Midnight Battle Prayer, a strategic intercession movement that gathers believers monthly to execute the "Verdict of the Decree" against the powers of darkness.
4. Mission: To transition the Body of Christ from "subjects of circumstance" to "Governors of Light" through deep foundational deliverance.

www.ingramcontent.com/pod-product-compliance
Lightning Source LLC
LaVergne TN
LVHW010839120826
845149LV00017B/3312

*9798995386186*